NEW YORK ENCOUNTER × 2019

Something TO START FROM

*This booklet contains transcripts, not reviewed by the speakers,
of talks given at New York Encounter 2019*

CROSS ROADS

Crossroads Cultural Center

HAB
Human Adventure Books

Transcriptions by Karen Kaffenberger
Copyediting and layout by Deep River Media, LLC

Human Adventure Books

Something to Start From
Proceedings of New York Encounter 2019
Crossroads Cultural Center
This edition © 2019 Human Adventure Books

Something TO START FROM

We are at the end of an epoch and we feel the need to rediscover our identity and somehow start again. But, having abandoned traditions, challenged norms, and rejected authorities, we are left with nothing but ourselves to make sense of it all. With no blueprint, the present is full of unease and the future appears enigmatic.

We are uncertain of the meaning of our lives, and so often feel confused, alone and isolated. Our collective days are filled by the pressures of success and conformity, along with the fear of being left behind. Failure seems irredeemable, mercy impossible. So, we often look for scapegoats or ways to escape. But tribal belonging or artificial realities are poor substitutes for the certainties we have lost.

At the same time, this very unease reveals *something* in us. *Something* that feels the lack, aches for meaning, and recognizes the truth, like a tuning fork vibrating for its single, unmistakable note. *Something* that makes us long to be looked at, listened to, understood, forgiven, valued just because we exist. *Something* that perceives a promise even within these challenging times and urges us to respond, to say "Here I am!", to seek justice, to build anew. An innermost, irreducible, decisive core marked by a stubborn expectation.

"HAS ANYONE EVER PROMISED US
ANYTHING? THEN WHY DO WE EXPECT
SOMETHING?" — CESARE PAVESE

Cover image: Henri Matisse, *Icarus*, 1946

CONTENTS

A Blossom in the Desert
Naomi and Ken Genuard, Miriam Huettner, Riro Manuscalco 13

An Epidemic of Loneliness
Kerry Cronin, Emily Esfahani Smith, Marcie Stokman....................... 23

"Do Not Be Afraid to Set Your Sights Higher" (Pope Francis)
Fr. Julián Carrón, Austen Ivereigh, Fr. José Medina............................ 41

Beyond the Moon...to the Farthest Reaches
Jonathan Lunine, Karin Öberg, Massimo Robberto............................ 59

An Irreducible Expectation
David Brooks, Fr. Javier Prades, John Zucchi 79

Poetry: The Language of Human Longing
Paul Mariani, Rita Simmonds 101

"When I Cannot Sing My Heart, I Can Only Speak My Mind"
John Waters 115

The Education of the Heart
Jon Balsbaugh, Archbishop Christophe Pierre, Holly Peterson.......... 129

"I Just Happen to Love Ordinary Things"
Francis Greene.. 145

Something is Happening Here
Richard F. Thomas, Robert George, Annemarie Bacich..................... 159

A New Beginning. Life in the Aftermath of a Massacre
Fr. Peter Cameron, Dawn Ford, Jenny Hubbard................................ 173

Born to Never Die
Enrico Petrillo, Angelo Carfi, Amy Hickl.. 191

A Blossom in the Desert

The stubborn expectation of the human heart: witnesses from Itauna (Brazil), Aleppo (Syria), and Boston (USA)

Introduction

"In the evolution of time and in the work of humankind, there is something, there is a phenomenon of something that is incorruptible, that cannot crumble away. Everyone speaks of it, and it is always new. The great Italian poet Leopardi called it the 'dominant thought.' This phenomenon is much greater than the sign, the ephemeral aspect of reality, that brings it about. Something bigger. It is the thirst for beauty. It is the thirst for truth. It is the thirst for happiness. It is the heart! The dominant thought, according to the totality of its meaning, is what the Bible calls 'heart': man perceives within that he is destined for happiness, for truth, for beauty, for goodness, for justice. Everyone judges based on these things; everyone, even if superficially! But what is most impressive is that this phenomenon cannot be removed: it cannot be removed! Ultimately, it is something that cannot be removed! In the middle of society's 'great ruin' — to use Dante's words — there is this impetuous, grandiose, powerful thing that raises itself. If this phenomenon dies, man dies of boredom."

~Fr. Luigi Giussani, notes from a talk on Giacomo Leopardi, Milan 1996

Naomi Genuard: At the bottom of the heart of every human being, from earliest infancy until the tomb, there is something that goes on indomitably expecting, in the teeth of all experience of crimes committed, suffered, and witnessed, that good and not evil will be done to him. It is this, above all, that is sacred in every human being. This profound, and childlike, and unchanging expectation of good in the heart is not what is involved when

Friday, February 15, 2019

we agitate for our rights. The motive which prompts a little boy to watch jealously to see if his brother has a slightly larger piece of cake arises from a much more superficial level of the soul. The word "justice" means two very different things according to whether it refers to the one, or the other, level. It is only the former one that matters.

Music

Fr. Ibrahim Alsabagh: Dearest brothers and sisters, may God give you peace. I am Fr. Ibrahim Alsabagh, a Franciscan friar who was sent in 2014 to Aleppo, in the middle of the disorder of the war, as the head of the Latin community of the city and as an Episcopal Vicar. At first glance, based on international news reports, it may appear that the situation in Syria is getting better. But in reality, the situation is still very critical. Three neighborhoods in Aleppo are still getting bombarded, and daily we hear about many dead and wounded because of the ongoing battle. This painful reality means our unemployment rate is over 70% and our poverty rate is over 80%. Many of our families are barely able to afford their daily bread, and for the ethnic and religious minorities, including Christians, things are even harder. When my superior asked me if I was ready to go and serve in Aleppo, I could not imagine what could be waiting for me. I am a Syrian born in Damascus, but I knew nothing about Aleppo until 2014. I served throughout the Middle East but never in Syria. For me, Aleppo was what I heard from the news. I could have simply refused to go because of the danger of death; nobody could force me to go or blame me if I didn't. What drove me to accept without hesitation was what my superior said: "Aleppo is in need. People are in need." I went to Aleppo with faith. I was certain that God's grace would give me something to start from. I went to Aleppo, taking with me only my trust and surrender to God. I carried my limited love toward Him and toward His people, and with my thirst to serve Him through every person in need. In fact, I am certain that charity is something that springs from an open heart, which leads one to make things he or she has never conceived of. This is how all the miracles I have witnessed in my four years in Aleppo have come about. For example, on a Sunday in October 2015, at 6:00 p.m., I was celebrating Mass when a missile hit a couple of our churches. It could have been a massacre, but miraculously, nobody died or was seriously hurt.

But the greater miracle happened the same day and the day after, when many parishioners, overcoming fear, came to clean and start repairing the church. And an even greater miracle happened the following Sunday, when people more numerous than usual came before Mass, and the shard of the missile was used as a vase for flowers to be offered in prayer for whomever launched the missile.

Another miracle is about Roula. Roula currently leads the catechism in our parish, and various other humanitarian projects of the Latin Church in Aleppo. She studied and graduated in France as a biologist, then got married in 1995 to Tony, a well-known lawyer in Aleppo. In 2008, Edma, their only daughter, was born. When this the war started in 2012 and Aleppo became a battlefield between the rebels and the regular army, she and her family decided to remain instead of moving to France. In 2014, the war became more violent, and while Roula's mother and brothers left Aleppo, she and Tony renewed their decision to remain. And hear of her bravery: nights of hunger, thirst, cold, and instability began. The condo where they were living was basically in the crossfire of the two armies, and often bullets were hitting the building. One day in 2015, after she crossed a street from her house, a missile hit the building, destroying it and killing 11 people. She understood that she was alive because of a miracle, and moved with her family to her parents' house in a quieter neighborhood of Aleppo called Villat. However, in 2016, Villat also started to be bombed, and missiles hit houses very close to theirs. One of their friends died. So, for the second time, frightened and full of sorrow, they moved to a house close to my parish, St. Francis. Ten months later, one morning a missile hit very close to St. Francis, exactly where her husband and daughter were supposed to arrive home. Terrified, Roula immediately called her daughter, Edma. At first, she didn't answer, then they started answering, but screaming. Roula ran desperately toward her house and saw the house almost destroyed. Edma was there, well and fearful, but alive. There was another miracle: while Edma was opening the door of her apartment, a missile hit the opposite side of the building, and the door protected Edma from the flying debris. With no other places to go in a town already destroyed by the war, they decided to remain. Thanks be to God, through the help of the Latin Church, her house was rebuilt very quickly. The Church cannot take away the Cross, but at least can make it lighter.

Roula, Tony, and Edma still live where they can see every day a destroyed city. Even in the midst of so much insecurity, bitterness, and fear, with nightmares tormenting her at night, Roula understood through prayer that she was called to remain in Aleppo, and to help the ever-growing number of undefended and terrified children whose families do not have the means to escape. And so, little by little, more and more parents are sending their children to the catechism program she directs. Approximately 250 at first, then 450 children, and today 900 youth. So, an oasis in the desert was born where children are healed. An oasis entrusted to the tender hands of a mother expert in suffering. But Roula also works in the parish center, open every day from 7:00 in the morning until midnight, welcoming whoever is in need. Sometimes as a nurse, sometimes as a firefighter, sometimes as a social worker, but always as a mother. Once, a needy old man came to the parish and started to talk about all of his sufferings. At the end he asked, "But who are you? I feel you are my mother." A mother radiates from your face, from your words. At the end of her very long day at the parish she is often exhausted, and then she goes home and takes care of her husband and daughter. Sometimes she is so tired that she cannot even sleep, but as she says when asked, she is glad in her heart, because she serves the Lord. When she is asked, Why did you remain? She answers, Because I have so many children in this city. I feel that the Lord wants me here. I have a mission right here in the midst of the ruins. And when someone asked, Where does all this gratuitousness come from? She answered, Why, people are praying, and I experience gratuitousness from Christ who gave me my life; I cannot help but give it back with the gift of myself. She started as a housewife, a woman hidden within the walls of her house. Excellent at cooking and keeping her house tidy. By opening herself to the needs of others, she has discovered at age 45 the many gifts of her life.

Let me finish with a wish. May God bless this Encounter 2019. Make all the participants go out after the end of this event of friendship enriched with something or someone to start from, to change our world and our reality. [*audience applause*]

Ken Genuard: That bitterness may turn to gladness. This is the inspiration, the criterion for all we do. We choose a movie instead of another. We choose a companionship instead of another, and so on. We resign ourselves to study, or to work, as long as at some point bitterness be turned into gladness. This is right; in fact, this is what reveals the nature of man. As Dante says: "Each one confusedly a good conceives / wherein the mind may rest and longeth for it." Everybody has a confused intuition of a good in which the mind may rest. Meaning a good in which the soul may reach complete satisfaction, corresponding to the word that can be pronounced with seriousness, only religiously, the word *happiness*. And this is the fundamental art of life. It is like the spark that ignites the engine, for every action and everybody strives, struggles for happiness. This is the nature of man according to the Christian tradition. Luigi Giussani.

Miriam Huettner: In August of 2017, a group of Ivy League professors published a letter addressed to incoming freshmen and to all students. And the content of this letter can be summed up in the phrase, "Think for yourself." They elaborated on this, saying, "Question dominant ideas, even when your friends or your professors insist on being treated as unquestionable. Be wary of conformism and groupthink."

One of my friends found this letter and shared it with us, a group of university students across North America. When we read the letter, we felt immediately that it was something that touched a part of us in our university life that is really dear to us, and that we all have questions about. In fact, we had many conversations about this letter, some that lasted over two hours, because we clearly had a lot of things to say and a lot of questions for these professors. We synthesized our thoughts in a letter of our own and sent it to the professors. At the end of that letter, we posed questions, and asked if they would like to meet with us to continue speaking. In the letter we explained how grateful we were to these professors for helping us recognize this mentality in the world, in the States, and especially on campuses. This groupthink, or certain ideas, can indeed be treated as unquestionable. But we also said that we were really grateful that they helped us realize that this tyranny of public opinion, as they phrased it, operates within ourselves first and foremost. We realize that it can be extremely difficult to think for ourselves. It's easy to go with the flow, and we have a fear that others, our friends especially, will identify us with what we think and say, reducing us only to those opinions, and so we often stay quiet and keep our questions and thoughts to ourselves, so as not to risk losing the respect of our friends. We also realized that, in order to think for ourselves, we have to understand what this self is, and in fact we talked a lot about the quote from Giussani that was just read, which is the definition of the heart, something that exists inside each of us: a general desire and need for truth, happiness, peace, justice. And in our many conversations, we said, If this is true, if every student in my class has the same basic need that I have, then dialogue or asking these questions about university life or anything, actually, can become not just ideas bouncing around, but instead a journey taken in common to get to the heart of these questions, to get to this true self that we all have. And often we realized — as I did in my experience — that it takes something or someone else, like a letter from professors, or a dialogue with a person who might hold extremely different opinions, to reawaken my sleepy heart or this thing inside of me that is kind of sleeping, so that I can really start to ask the questions that matter in my life: Why am I here? What am I doing? How can I live? While I was in college, the questions of conformism and groupthink or all these questions in general were definitely on my mind, but by and large, for four whole years I stayed silent. I had this fear that my friends would put me in a box that I didn't think at all represented me, and often I felt suffocated and didn't really know what to do with that, and I didn't know quite where to start.

But then a couple of my friends showed me this letter, and asked me to think about it, and take part in it. And we started talking together and meeting with the professors. I think I actually didn't realize it was possible for me to start living these questions and talking to professors in this way. It's not that I'm not afraid anymore, but that I have people who are really helping me grow and live, and I wouldn't have done this if it weren't for these friends. I'll share with you a couple of things that the professors have said in our conversations. After meeting with one of them, he sent us an email thanking us and said, "It is exceedingly rare that I have the chance to talk so openly about such fundamental and important questions. It is also genuinely encouraging to see that there are students out there who are so engaged by such questions that they will travel to speak with professors about them. You all made quite an impression on me."

One of the professors said that, in his perception, the most difficult thing today is to see what's directly in front of our eyes, and he thinks that in universities today there's an unknown or perhaps hidden goal to convince students that what we see in front of our eyes isn't real. And he added that we have no way to discuss what a human should be and how to live, because we don't agree on any common foundation anymore. The belief that many in our culture hold is that we are the sovereign of our life. We can decide exactly who we want to be, and how, and we decide what reality is. In meeting with these professors, my experience has been, I would say, a bit of the opposite, in the sense that I need the professor who has another, different idea. I need someone to provoke me. I can only make sense of myself in the context of a greater whole and in relation to others. I don't decide what this life or what this reality is, I don't create it or make it, but somehow it's something that comes to me and I can discover it or not. I can really see it or not. One of the professors also said to me, "If you've graduated from college without ever being offended, you should ask for your money back." We really should be challenged, we should be offended. Education should be painful. He said we need a master who can guide us.

This is a bit of what I've found in asking questions of others who are farther along the path: I need someone to follow, I need someone to guide me, and I cannot find my way without a road. But realizing that I also have this heart, and it really is the way that Giussani and Leopardi define it: to recognize the road that is in front of me. [*audience applause*]

Riro Manuscalco: What makes a prisoner stay and work when he could try to escape? What makes people like Fr. Ibrahim Alsabagh remain in Aleppo and keep building, risking their lives when they could run? And what makes a young student like Miriam challenge the common mentality and start knocking on professors' doors? Where does that cry come from? Where does that pain come from? What is the yearning we heard in the cello piece that Marcel Krasner played for us? What is the thread that ties together all these teeny, tiny dots, which are so far apart from each other? There is something, and it is that something that we want to get to know during these days: keeping our eyes open, keeping our ears open, and keeping our hearts open. We worked all these months, a long journey that brought us here tonight, carrying with us Cesare Pavese's question. I don't know if you remember it: "Has anyone ever promised us anything?

Then why do we expect something?" Has anyone ever promised anything to those people in Aleppo? To those of us here? Then why do we expect something? Because we *do* expect something, and we can't help it.

Fr. Giussani, commenting on Pavese's question, wrote that perhaps Pavese didn't realize that expectation is the very structure of our nature, is the essence of our soul. It is not something calculated, it is given, for the promise is at the origin. From the very origin of our creation, He who has made man has also made him a promise. Structurally man awaits. Structurally he is a beggar. Structurally life is promised, and that is why we're here, kicking off the 2019 New York Encounter.

Thank you all so much for giving me time to talk. I love you, and wish you a happy new year. God bless.

An Epidemic of Loneliness

*Living, dating, and dying in a time of isolation. With **Kerry Cronin**, Associate Director of the Lonergan Institute at Boston College; **Emily Esfahani Smith**, Author; and moderated by **Marcie Stokman**, Founder of the Well-Read Mom reading group*

Introduction

"A terrible sense of solitude overcomes the human being in the face of a destiny devoid of all meaning. Solitude, in fact, does not signify to be alone, but the absence of a meaning. You could stand in the middle of a million people and still be as alone as you can possibly be, if those million people present have no meaning for you. That solitude which we often lament in our life with others, betrays our misunderstanding of its meaning. We live together failing to recognize what unites us. Thus even the smallest offense becomes a pretense for breaking down the bonds of trust. In this way, solitude becomes an exasperating social climate, and sadly is the characteristic face of today's society. The celebrated name of Teilhard de Chardin comes to mind with the tremendous statement that the greatest danger which today's humanity needs to fear is not a catastrophe which comes from out there somewhere, a stellar catastrophe, neither is it famine, nor even disease; rather it is spiritual malady, which is the most terrible malady: it is to remain 'without the taste for life.'"

~Luigi Giussani, *The Religious Sense*, McGill, 1997, pages 85-86

❖   ❖   ❖   ❖   ❖

Marcie Stokman: Welcome, everybody. I'm Marcie Stokman and I'll be moderating this event. If we finish early, there will be time for questions, so keep that in mind. Volunteers will come around with microphones. To my left is Dr. Kerry Cronin, Associate Director of the Lonergan Institute at Boston College and Faculty Fellow at the Center for Student Formation. For the past 20 years, she has taught in the Boston College Interdisciplinary Perspectives Program, a Philosophy and Theology program in the "great books" tradition. Additionally, she works extensively with undergraduates in retreat programs at Boston College and is a regular speaker on college campuses, addressing topics of student culture and formation. Kerry is also known for her decade-long studies in the area of human affectivity and dating.

Emily Esfahani Smith is a journalist and the author of *The Power of Meaning: Finding Fulfillment in a World Obsessed With Happiness*. She is also an editor at the Manhattan Institute. Her articles and essays have appeared in the *Wall Street Journal, New York Times, The Atlantic, The New Criterion,* and other publications. In 2017, she delivered a main stage TED talk, "There's More to Life Than Being Happy." Smith was born in Zurich, Switzerland, and grew up in Montreal, Canada. She now lives in Washington, D.C.

Today we are experiencing what many call an epidemic in loneliness, and I imagine this topic resonates with everybody here. We recognize a new kind of loneliness in our culture. Last year, I attended three funerals where the cause of death was suicide. This is a tragic increase; something is happening in our culture. There's a growing inability to establish fulfilling relationships, and I think we all sense this. One aspect of this inability is played out in the progressive decline of dating in our culture. It's confusing — what constitutes dating now? How do young people go about this process? That's why a lot of you were drawn to this particular event, because it's an issue that affects all of us.

So, Kerry: you started the Dating Project. What is that? How did this come about? What did you see in the lives of your students at Boston College, and in the culture at large, that brought about the Dating Project?

Kerry Cronin: About 17 or 18 years ago I had a great conversation with a group of Boston College seniors. We were just talking about life and life after graduation, that sort of thing. I stumbled into the question of dating.

I said, "Well, what are you going to do when you graduate? Are you going to pick up with people you've been dating, or what's going to happen?" And they all sort of looked at me like I was speaking Greek, and I don't know how to speak Greek. I said, "You know what I mean, right? The people you're dating..." And they said to me, "Oh no, we don't date anymore. We just...we don't know how to do that. That's crazy. But hooking up is great — you know, that kind of thing."

Around campus I would run into people and start asking them about dating and hooking up — and I got too much information in a lot of cases. [*audience laughter*] It was kinda scary. Then maybe a semester or two after that, I started talking to a group of seniors in a capstone class I was teaching. I asked them to go on a date: to ask somebody out in person and go on a date. I figured it was an easy assignment, but I soon discovered that it wasn't. And that first semester it took them months, and most of them weren't even able to complete the assignment. So after that I made it a mandatory assignment. [*audience laughter*] I used to say to students, "I'll flunk you in this class if you don't ask somebody out." Which is a little shady, but...

Stokman: Did class size go up?

Cronin: You know, at first I announced it because I'm fair, and didn't want to get fired. I announced it during the drop/add period, and so a bunch of students immediately left the class. But then other students came in and it filled up, and now it's at the point where I have students regularly say, "I'm taking your class so you'll make me go on a date." [*audience laughter*] I thought, Or, you could just ask somebody on a date. I don't know, but okay. [*audience laughter*]

But to the question. What I saw struck me as an important question: What's going on? But then this quickly became connected to me and other faculty noticing that the levels of depression and anxiety in our college students today is just off the charts. It's really frightening.

Stokman: So over the last 10 years you've seen an increasing distance in the students. Can you describe this distance, and the possibilities you see in overcoming this distance?

Cronin: We all know that college kids are so very connected on social media, right? They're constantly connecting to people; and yet, you feel that they don't really have any deep connections, or that they struggle with deep connections. They want them but they don't know how to go about them. I remember talking to a young man who had been in my class: he had come by to talk to me about something, and he said, "I just had my 21st birthday the other day." And I said, "That's great! Congratulations! Happy birthday!" And he said, "Yes, it was great: I went out with 32 of my closest friends." "Did you say 32?" "Yes." So I said, "You don't know what the word 'closest' means, right?" And when I started talking to him about those friendships, I realized they were more or less the social equivalent of a fist-bump. Nothing substantial. When I speak to college students around the country, what I hear is a grinding, low-level despair. A kind of grinding despair and lack of hope about it all working out. About how to figure all this out in a culture that doesn't help them anymore. We know from research that most college students believe in God but also feel distant from God. I wonder which of those distances came first: our distance from each other or our distance from God? In which direction does that go? It's a daunting problem, but I am really confident from the responses I get from college students that they are craving help, they want help, and thus help is possible.

Stokman: So even with a lot of connections, a lot of friends at this birthday party, there weren't a lot of real relationships. Emily, you wrote a book entitled *The Power of Meaning*. It's wonderful, thank you for writing it. Finding fulfillment in a world obsessed with happiness — how did your interest in the problem of meaning come about?

Emily Esfahani Smith: Thank you all for being here. It's so wonderful to be with this community and with Marcie and Kerry. So: this low-level despair that you talk about — that phrase really resonated with me. I grew up, I think, like a lot of people, in a household that was spiritual and religious. My parents were Sufis. Sufism is a mystical branch of Islam. The poet Rumi was a Sufi. Actually, we lived in a Sufi meeting house my parents administered, so there were Sufis who came to our home twice a week to meditate. As a child, that was a very enchanting experience, to be in this world of mystical seekers who had clear answers to the big questions: What is the meaning of life? It's something you call God, you call it the sacred, the transcendent. And living a meaningful life was about doing certain things to get closer to that higher reality, whether it was meditating, praying, doing acts of service, or practicing loving kindness. That really stayed with me. Eventually, though, as I got older, we moved out of this Sufi meeting house — this was in Montreal by the way — and we came to the United States. Without that daily grounding of Sufism, that presence of this higher, transcendent thing to strive towards, I began to wonder: What is this all about it? Is it possible to live a meaningful life without religion, outside of a spiritual context? In college, this led me to study philosophy, and in graduate school to study positive psychology, which is a field of psychology concerned with the ancient philosophical questions: What is a good life? What is virtue? How can we all be happy and find meaning? What I discovered was that there's so much emphasis on happiness in our culture. We receive these messages from the culture to be happy, pursue happiness, and that if we just do that, it will fill us up. But we have all these people, especially young people, who *are* doing that. They're on this quest, chasing success, riches, doing what they think they're supposed to do to be happy. Yet there's this rising tide of despair, not just among the young but among everyone. The statistics show that, and we can talk about that if you're interested.

In the positive psychology program, I came across research about meaning, which finally gave me a language to understand why the happiness zeitgeist was not resonating. The research showed that what actually brings people fulfillment and fills this kind of existential vacuum is feeling connected to something beyond yourself: being part of something bigger, feeling like your life matters and is significant. That really resonated, so I just started writing about it, and I received a large response like with Kerry's dating class. I think it suggests there's a hunger for serious engagement with these questions. So many of our traditional sources of meaning, and venues for discussing meaning, are no longer part of people's daily lives, and so they're yearning for ways to discuss these things. I think your class, and the things that I'm writing — these give them the necessary venues. But that yearning is definitely there.

Stokman: So you're saying that some of the places where we used to access meaning are no longer there. Can you speak more about that? And also, in your book you write: "When people can't answer the why of existence they can conclude that life is meaningless." Can you speak more to the "why" of existence?

Smith: Definitely. So, it's an interesting audience. I wonder if people in this audience feel this way, but I think that if you pluck your average secular person from a city like New York, or a college campus like Boston College, you'll find that they're probably not going to church, or temple, or mosque, or whatever. They're distant from the communities that ground people's lives. Kids leave home to go to college and for work, and they often do not return. A sense of tradition, ritual: these things that for thousands of years programmed meaning into our lives, and organized our lives, are just not really part of the day-to-day experience of lived existence anymore. That's what I'm talking about when I say that these traditional forms of meaning are not there. The absence of community and religion and transcendence and ritual — people are forced to find meaning on their own, and that can be a very daunting challenge. Viktor Frankl, the Holocaust survivor, talks about how the yearning people have for meaning is as important and vital for our psychological and spiritual well-being as food and water are for our physical being. And so, without that, people give up hope and eventually begin to despair. Without the answers that were previously given to us, or at least without considering their possibility, through religion, through community, and in tradition — we're left to find that "why" on our own. Viktor Frankel wrote *Man's Search for Meaning*, a beautiful book about his experiences in the concentration camps. The whole message of that book is that the people who were able to endure this horrendous form of suffering — the ones more apt to survive the general degradation of camp life — were the ones who had a "why," some reason to go on living. You find this in the modern research on meaning, as well: that people who have a sense of meaning in life actually live longer, are more likely to use preventative health services, and take better care of themselves. And it also suggests that the reason is, when you have that "why" you have a reason to move into the future. The future feels good, so you want to preserve yourself for it.

Stokman: Meaning affects the way we behave.

Smith: Yes.

Stokman: Our sense of meaning changes our behavior. Before expanding on what each of you has said, can you each speak about the root cause that you see for the epidemic of loneliness in our culture? What would you say is the root cause?

Smith: That is a hard question. Ssome of the research I did for my writing suggests that, over the past 200 years but probably even longer, there's been a great shift in the values of Western culture towards individualism and away from community. There are many interesting studies that look at how language use has changed over time. If you look back 200 years ago, there was more use of the words "we" and "community" and "us," as well as the concepts associated with community: duty, for example, responsibility, and giving. In books and art, in newspaper articles, more of these words appeared. Today you have more words like "I," "me," "unique," "creative," "personal" — things that express a focus on the self. One of the studies that resonated with me talks about how this change in values overlapped with increasing urbanization and industrialization; I think there's a kind of sociological story about how as people moved to the cities and away from home, the focus shifted to their own careers, and consequently there was a loss of the community spirit.

Cronin: I notice this when I come to New York. I'm always so excited, but then you can be anonymous with so many people, right within ten feet of you. The root of loneliness is a really hard question. Many of us don't feel lonely when we're alone, so it's much more an existential problem than a social problem. It's hard to get at that with young adults, because our fear of talking about loneliness is really palpable. I know so many students who are trying to argue their way into bringing a comfort animal to campus — they all want to bring dogs to campus. And guess what? It's because a dog looks at you. The dog keeps looking at your face, wondering why you're not feeding it [*audience laughter*]. But to have another being looking in your eyes, it's very powerful and healing and consoling. So often I watch students in the cafeterias, or sitting, and they're looking at their phones, and then they look up and no one is looking back. No one is ever looking them in the eye. And when students go on my dating assignments, one of the things they're really nervous about is looking someone in the eye for an hour, because we don't do it anymore. I think there's a biological and existential issue there.

Stokman: My nieces and nephews visited me over Christmas and I asked some questions about dating. One of my nephews said the rules have changed. "What are the rules?" I asked. And he said guys don't know how to go about it, and fear getting in trouble either way. Do they take the lead? Does that offend? They have no idea what the rules are, and it seems that in this culture dating is a real risk. Would you agree with that?

Cronin: Oh, absolutely. My first-year students just got their dating assignment the other day. They are *terrified*. Immediately, my office hours schedule became packed. They don't want to talk about Thomas Hobbes, they want to talk about dating. They are terrified. I often say to them, "Look, in so many parts of our lives, effort correlates to success, but not in this one." We're very risk averse, because guess what? That's evidence that we're human. We live in a consumer capitalist society: we just want to push and work hard on our own individual projects. To ask somebody else to see us, and ratify us, and tell us that we're valuable and that we mean something is really terrifying. I often say to students, "I just want you to go for a coffee with them. I don't want you to necessarily find a soulmate. I mean, that would be great if you did, but could you just ask somebody out for a cup of coffee and say, 'I just want to get to know you'?" I have the students come back and talk to each other about how hard it was to ask somebody out, what happened, what were the funny things that happened, and then they write up a reflection. Almost all of them say, "I couldn't believe how much the person was asking me about myself." And I think, Why does that surprise you? That shouldn't be surprising. You're fascinating, you're interesting, and you're great to be around.

Stokman: But even having a few rules gives people permission to take a risk? Why would you say they should take the risk? To the young people out there, why should they want to...

Cronin: Well, to pass the class! [*audience laughter*]

Stokman: But is it worth taking the risk? We're more fragile.

Cronin: Sure. And to your nephew's point, the rules are gone. One of the things I realized when I started thinking about this — I had just been reading some of Jared Diamond's work, and Jane Jacobs' final book, *Dark Age Ahead*, which is a great book on the loss of social script, which is the case with dating. The social script has been lost, so nobody knows what the rules are. Risk is fine if you know what the rules are, right? So when you go hiking or skiing or something, and it gives you one diamond, two diamonds, three diamonds — you know what the risk is and you're anticipating, "Okay, I'm going to have to come up with this much of a skill set. Am I ready for a green trail, or a black diamond trail?" You've got to know. But because we don't know what dating is about anymore, we can't assess the risk going in. What I say now is: This is just a Level One day. This is reconnaissance work only, this is just finding out, this is information gathering. Then they think, Okay, alright, maybe I can do this. If you can lower the stakes and give them rules — by the second semester I realized I had to give them actual directions — then they can do it and they can blame me. That's fine; this crazy lady is making me go on a date.

Stokman: Emily, you wrote about the need we have to live beyond ourselves, to experience meaning, and that also takes risk. Can you speak to the risk involved in living a life of meaning?

Smith: What you're saying, Kerry, is really corresponding with me. In my book I write about how, for most people, the central source of meaning in their lives are their relationships and communities that give them a sense of belonging, which is really important for a meaningful life. It's one way that we go beyond, right? The risk, though, is that you are emotionally exposed, you make yourself vulnerable to other people. I have a younger brother in college and I remember very well that period in my own life, too. You're taught from a young age — especially if you go to a place like Boston College or you live in a city like New York — that you're given the script for how to be successful, how to achieve all this stuff. But you're no longer given any script for how to love well, how to lead a meaningful life. Then you reach adulthood and have to do it, you have to figure out if this is something you want to devote yourself to. There are no rules and you have been so good at succeeding in all the endeavors of your life; you've never really experienced failure, and probably your parents haven't let you, because they're managing your life. These might be the first times you've ever really encountered failure and rejection, and that's unbearable for a lot of people. I wrote an article about this recently. I'm so drawn to this topic because we're so afraid to show others who we really are. Whether it's through asking them on a date or what have you. It's really important to know that when you do this, people actually love it, they're really drawn to it. The research shows this; your anecdotal experience will show it. I experimented with that this past year, a very difficult year: I was vulnerable and shared with my friends and with mentors, and was amazed by the degree to which it brought me closer to a community and deepened those bonds of connection. It created belonging and brought meaning to my life at a time when I really felt unmoored.

Stokman: One college student told me that the loneliest place on campus — and Kerry, you kind of alluded to this — is the Student Center. She said, "We only have each other to look at, and so most of us look down." This brings us into a proposal, a need for a proposal to look at something together. It's easier to be with other students if we have something to look at together, because loneliness is not just overcome by being in the same place. The word "belonging" — can we talk about that a little bit? What would each of you say about this need to belong?

Smith: I think belonging is kind of the magic that makes relationships worth your while. We will have a lot of relationships, people that we interact with, people at work, people in our own family — but a sense of belonging might not always be there. Just because you have a relationship with someone doesn't mean that belonging exists. So, belonging, as I understand it, is being in a relationship where you really feel valued for who you are intrinsically, and where you value other people for who they are intrinsically. I think that's a really important, intrinsic piece of it, because so many of us are in relationships where we're valued for what we do, what we achieve, who we hate, and not really for who we are. There's something about seeing another person and accepting their intrinsic worth. If you're religious, this could be their soul, their atman, or whatever. Loving that piece of God or the divine in each person. I think that's the core of belonging.

Stokman: And when there is a sense of belonging, there's increased meaning.

Smith: Yes exactly. There's so much research on this, and I'm sure that people's experience can speak to this as well. When you feel a sense of belonging, there's something about knowing you matter to others that makes you understand your own life is mattering. I'll tell you about one psychology study that showed this in a bit of a cruel way. They had all these college students come into the lab, and they basically told them they had to mingle with one another. They told some of them that there's going to be a second socializing experience — and oh, by the way, all the people you met want to talk to you again. And then they told the other half that, sorry, actually none of the people you met want to talk to you again — you are just that awful. [*audience laughter*] But the people who were made to feel rejected and ostracized not only rated their own lives less meaningful, but they rated life in general less meaningful. So there's a truly powerful connection between this kind of existential sense of meaning and feeling like you belong in the world and have value to others.

Stokman: But if you feel you don't belong, what steps can you take to increase inner understanding of belonging and experience of belonging?

Smith: Belonging isn't just a feature of a relationship — and this is one of the things I learned as I researched my book and spoke to people — it is a choice that you make and it's something that exists, can exist, in moments between people. On dates, for example, where there is an alchemy that happens. A friend of mine told me a story that will illustrate this. My friend, Jonathan, lives in New York City on the Upper West Side, and every morning he has a routine: he goes and buys a newspaper from a street vendor on the corner near the subway. You can imagine: it's New York, it's rush hour, it's busy, and these two people have every incentive to rush through this transaction, this exchange of goods and money. But they both take a moment to slow down to talk to each other, to treat each other like human beings, and over the years they've gotten to know one another and ask about one another's children, wish each other happy birthdays, and they always leave that encounter feeling elevated. That was a meaningful connection, a moment of grace that lifted them up for the rest of the day.

Well, one time, Jonathan went to go buy the newspaper and he realized he didn't have the right change, and the vendor said don't worry about it, this time it's on me. But Jonathan felt uncomfortable with that, so he went to a store and bought something he didn't need to make change. When he returned and gave the money to the vendor, the vendor drew back; he was hurt. He had been trying to do something to raise the stakes of intimacy and belonging in their friendship, but Jonathan had rejected that bid for affection. I think of that story a lot. How easy it is to build up belonging, and also how easy it is to knock it down in ways that we probably all do all the time: checking our phones on a date, or at dinner with our spouse. But just as easy as it is to knock it down, it's also easy to build it up by seeking out and cultivating those moments of connection. The next time Jonathan saw the vendor, he brought him a cup of tea as a way to apologize and restore their connection, and they continue to share that moment each day. It's really putting yourself out there a little bit, being a little vulnerable, and finding those connections in relationships that you have with close ones, but also with people more distant.

Stokman: But you're also saying that nothing is insignificant in these little interactions, and we can repair them and be intentional, intentional about greater belonging in our lives.

Smith: Exactly. I was just speaking at a high school the other day, and the woman who was driving me around is on faculty at the high school, and she was telling me how amazing it is to her that, years later, students will come to her and say, "I just wanted to let you know it meant so much to me that day, fall semester, when you asked me how my exam went," or when she said they did a really good job in the play. It really struck her, because to her, she was just being her normal self, but for them it was somebody they respected saying, "I care for you, I see you." She didn't realize she had that effect. We all can have that effect.

Stokman: Kerry, would you say there's a connection between belonging to a community and dating?

Cronin: Oh, goodness, absolutely. But let me hold off on that for just a minute, because I have something to add about the other question. I was watching Emily's TED talk the other day, which is fantastic — you all should watch her TED talk. I really loved what you said about belonging on the cheap, too, that there's something really powerful about belonging at all of these different levels and niches in our lives. It made me think of a Jesuit at Boston College, Father Paul McNellis, who spent some time in the military, and in Vietnam. When he talks about friendship, he talks a lot about the type of friendship that forms when you have a purpose or a project, and you're both looking at the same goal, you're both working toward the same thing. And that can be wonderful, but it can also be belonging on the cheap. I talk to students who come back from wonderful service trips, or have worked on a service project together, and then they don't know how to develop community that really sustains those connections. They don't know how to do it, they're college students, so what they do is just drink together. I say to them, "Isn't it strange that you went on this amazing service trip, you had these deep connections on questions of faith, justice, and solidarity, but then you come back and you can't figure out how to sustain the community of belonging?" I think this goes to your next question, about dating: it feels too risky if you don't have regular experiences of people saying, "You." If you feel like it always has to be about something else and never about you, then the step into dating and a romantic relationship feels like some other planet.

Stokman: Okay, to both of you: taking into account the Encounter's title, "Something to Start From," what are your final thoughts about where we can start from to address the epidemic of loneliness and dating?

Cronin: One of the things I have discovered in these years of giving my students dating assignments is that mostly what they're excited about after they've done the assignment is *not* that they have found somebody to marry. I mean, that has happened, but mostly what they experience is their own social courage. Their own courage to ask for what they really want, and to ask themselves what they really desire and what they really fear. What I often say to them is, it's small acts of courage that we need, it's small acts of social courage and paying attention when we miss the mark. I often tell my students to remember what Aristotle says. He spends a lot of time in his *Ethics* telling us what courage is not, because he says most people get it wrong. Courage is not recklessness; it's not running into a burning building. Courage is knowing what's worth fearing and what's worth pursuing, and habituating yourself to pursue what's really worth pursuing, and to avoid what is really worth fearing and what is soul-damaging. Small acts of courage are the "something" we can start from, I think.

Stokman: Even with dating, you say not everyone is called to marriage, but everyone is called to relationship. And so taking that risk launches us into relationship. Emily?

Smith: There's a study I keep thinking about. I'm sure you're familiar with it, there was a *New York Times* article written about it that went super-viral. Perhaps you all have read it. It was called, "To Fall in Love With Anyone, Do This." The woman who wrote the article went through and did what a study made college students do: sit with each other for an hour and ask each other a series of increasingly intimate questions, and at the very end they are supposed to stare into each other's eyes for a few minutes — which goes back to Kerry's point about eyes. The questions were of increasing intimacy. The first one was, like: If you could have anyone over to dinner, who would it be? The second one was something like: Tell me about a bad dream you had, or What was your relationship with your mother and father like? The most intimate question would be something similar to: Tell me something about you that nobody knows, and tell me something that you're struggling with right now. Believe it or not, my husband and I went through and did some of them together. I think what is so powerful about those questions is that they get you to cut right to what really matters and have a conversation that's really deep, and in which you both feel it's safe to be vulnerable. I think that for so many people, this is such a powerful way to build meaning in the encounters we have with one another. Where you see the other person as a real, embodied, three-dimensional being. Another example would be something like this: there's a wonderful organization called StoryCorps, which has you go into a booth and be interviewed by somebody you know — for example, a daughter will interview a mother, or two friends will interview each other. And they ask questions they ordinarily wouldn't ask one another. Your daughter might ask you, "Mom, when did you know you first fell in love with dad?" And it produces these beautiful conversation transcripts that deepen that relationship. People who do this say, "Oh, my God, we've known each other for all these years, how come we haven't talked about this stuff before?" If you just Google the website, they have all kinds of prompts and things like that. They even have an app that let's you record a conversation with somebody and it gets archived in the Library of Congress. So it's always there, this piece of your history. [*audience laughter*]

Stokman: To lessen loneliness and increase meaning, we need belonging, we need to risk, we need to be vulnerable, we need community. We can open it up now for some questions from the audience.

Speaker #1: Many of us believe that what is meaningful in our life informs how we date and the relationships we build and maintain. Viktor Frankl went into the concentration camps an agnostic, but his experience led him to believe that God objectively existed, and eventually he became a practicing Christian. Is there any research showing that people who are practicing Christians or Jews are more or less lonely than others?

Smith: I can't point to a specific study, but I do think that the general sense of it is, people who are actively religious are less lonely because they have a sense of community in their religion. Also, if they happen to be married or have a family, having that shared value system helps them find more connectedness with one another. You have so many people who are married but feel lonely in their marriage, and having this kind of transcendent architecture around them, I think, makes it easier to feel more connected. Because when all the things in life that can pull you apart — like work, or whatever — start distracting you, you can ground into those values. You mentioned dogs earlier, and I think one reason why dogs are such a solution is because it's a form of unconditional love. In religion, at least in Christianity, Judaism, and Islam, there's this idea that God loves you no matter what. There's a sense that something about me is still valuable and even eternally valuable, and this is reassuring and a balm against the loneliness that would otherwise come.

Speaker #2: Emily, what brought this question to mind was just watching you. You look for all the world about 22 years old, and you speak like a 75-year-old sage, which to me brings up the question of age. At an ontological level, do you see this reticence we have toward relating? Does it change with the individual over time? It's hard to believe, but as I've gotten older — I'm 60 now — I've been accused of being more direct than I was when I was younger. We have nursing homes full of lonely elderly people. Is this another bulge in the population, like the baby boomer era, where we're setting ourselves up for an even worse collection of lonely people in the future, all elderly?

Smith: I interviewed Camille Paglia recently, a provocateur in academia. She made a really interesting point about the rule of elderly people in our society. She says that in the Agrarian Age, as you got older, you had more status in society. The idea was that these were people who had wisdom to offer and that they would live in community with their children. They would be taking care of their grandchildren and having a really valuable role to play. Today, it's not like that. As you get older, you turn your kids into caretakers instead. It's just different. Older people now feel like they are a burden to others, and I think that's really sad. I mean, my mom is from Iran and my grandmother, her mother, used to live with us for half the year when she was spending more time here in the States. It always struck me that to my mom — and then to her other sisters who my grandmother also lived with — they never really thought of themselves as caretakers. Their mom was just kind of living with them, and it was wonderful to have her around. Maybe not so much for my dad. [*audience laughter*] He loved her, it was great. They had a wonderful relationship.

Speaker #3: Help me to understand what…I mean, I don't mean to be rude, but what is the point of this talk? Because every time I hear this sort of messaging, I just think it's a bunch of people from another generation patronizing me, saying, "Oh, we did it right, and you should be doing it better." Like, what am I missing? How do I not think of it in that light and also, what am I doing right? It just doesn't seem like I'm accompanied by anybody, it's just like, "You should be doing better and here are the steps to do better." It seems kind of a Band-Aid solution to a real problem.

Cronin: When I visit campuses to talk to students about dating and hook-up culture, the schools will often ask me to speak to faculty and staff at lunchtime, and then speak to the young adults at night, because that's when they want to talk. And usually I say to faculty and staff, "Look, we've got a lot of young people who are with us, and we're trying to accompany them on journeys of discernment. But we often ask them to do all the integration work of their education, while we don't do any of that. We sit in our academic silos; I don't ever talk to anybody who's not in the Philosophy Department. And, to your point, I think you're absolutely right. I don't want to sound like I'm saying, "Oh, these young people just haven't figured it out." It's just that, culturally, we've lost a lot of the modes of belonging, the modes of community, and the script that made it easier to work your way through loneliness and just have it be a facet of your life and not something that tips you into really significant depression and anxiety. This is a cultural project. It's a conversation we all need to have, young and old. As for your last question, we're all in this together trying to figure it out. You mention Band-Aids. I think of what Pope Francis says: "First you have to tend to the wounds." People are wounded, and sometimes Band-Aids are needed; but you're right: there's a larger, systemic, really complex set of conditions that are leaving a lot of us feeling isolated and alone, and existentially fraught and existentially fragile. In a world of so much connectivity, we should not feel unseen. I apologize if any of us sounded like we think that young people created these problems. My college students did not create these problems. They are trying to find a way through it, and my job is to companion with people. This is a problem for us all.

Stokman: Our time is up. Thank you so much for coming. This is the beginning of a much-needed conversation.

"Do Not Be Afraid to Set Your Sights Higher" (Pope Francis)

*Discovering Pope Francis' vision for a new evangelization. With **Fr. Julián Carrón**, President of the Fraternity of Communion and Liberation; **Austen Ivereigh**, Writer and Journalist; and moderated by **Fr. José Medina**, U.S. coordinator of Communion and Liberation*

Introduction

"Do not be afraid of holiness. It will take away none of your energy, vitality or joy. On the contrary, you will become what the Father had in mind when He created you, and you will be faithful to your deepest self. To depend on God sets us free from every form of enslavement and leads us to recognize our great dignity. We see this in Saint Josephine Bakhita: abducted and sold into slavery at the tender age of seven, she suffered much at the hands of cruel masters. But she came to understand the profound truth that God, and not man, is the true Master of every human being, of every human life. This experience became a source of great wisdom for this humble daughter of Africa."

~Pope John Paul II, Homily at the Mass of Canonization, October 1, 2000

"To the extent that each Christian grows in holiness, he or she will bear greater fruit for our world. The bishops of West Africa have observed that 'we are being called in the spirit of the New Evangelization to be evangelized and to evangelize through the empowering of all you, the baptized, to take up your roles as salt of the earth and light of the world wherever you find yourselves.' Do not be afraid to set your sights higher, to allow yourself to be loved and liberated by God. Do not be afraid to let yourself be guided by the Holy Spirit. Holiness does not make you less human, since it is an encounter between your weakness and the power of God's grace. For in the words of León Bloy, when all is said and done, 'the only great tragedy in life is not to become a saint.'"

~Pope Francis, Apostolic Exhortation *Gaudete and Exsultate*

❖ ❖ ❖ ❖ ❖

Fr. José Medina: Good afternoon everybody, and welcome to this event. I have great hopes and expectations that it will be beautiful, and will offer an opportunity to get to know Pope Francis. We live in a time of deep crisis and fluidity. A lot of change, a lot of questions, and one thing that we will not do today is talk about what is happening now. We are not CNN, we are not going to be talking about what is happening now. We're talking about something that is rather more important, that is, to give you the possibility from first accounts of people who have read and have met Pope Francis personally, to hear from them who he is, to hear from them what he has in his heart, to hear from them what he sees. To do so, we have three panelists with us. We have Archbishop Pierre. He is the U.S. Nuncio and a dear friend to us from his times as Nuncio in Uganda, and we are very grateful for his continuous encouragement and fatherhood towards us. We have Austen Ivereigh, who is now Fellow Contemporary in Church History at Campion Hall in Oxford — that is a beautiful title, Austen, very, very beautiful — and a journalist and writer. He wrote a very beautiful book on Pope Francis called *The Great Reformer* that I very much enjoyed. To my right, Father Julián Carrón. He is the President of the Fraternity of Communion and Liberation, a fellowship in the Church to which I belong and therefore have a great affection for. Our intention for the next hour is to have a conversation about who this man is. To try to understand better why, in this particular time in history, the Holy Spirit has given us this man in particular; not other popes, but this man in particular. So, without further ado, I would like to begin a dialogue by asking this very simple question to Austen: What is he like?

Austen Ivereigh: Thank you so much, Fr. Jose, it's lovely to be with you. I apologize for my strange English accent. [*audience laughter*] I hope you understand me. What is Pope Francis like? Well, when you meet him — and everybody who has met him and spent time with him will say the same thing — what strikes you is his astonishing graciousness. He creates this space for you to inhabit in front of him where he makes you feel you're very special, and he's a very ordinary person. In a strange way, he is an ordinary person and he likes people to see him that way and not as Superman. My biography of him is called *The Great Reformer*, and I think — he never said this to me directly — but I think he slightly has a problem with the title, because it implies he's a kind of Superman. In fact, he is a remarkable human being of extraordinary intelligence and all the other things that we admire in people, but actually his humility is really what is so striking; that he depends not on his own power and on his own gifts, but ultimately on the Holy Spirit, so that his task is to create space for the Spirit to act. When you're with him, that's the invitation he makes to you. When I met him — I'll just say one more thing — when I met him, and I won't go into too much detail, but I had a meeting with him, it was a recent time. I had two thoughts in my head. One of them was, Wow, you're talking to the pope! And the other is, you can say whatever you like to him; you can ask him whatever you want, you can say whatever you want. He produces an enormous sense of freedom in you, and I've often wondered since that meeting what it would have been like to meet Jesus Christ, and I think it would have been the same sensation; you had a freedom.

Archbishop Christophe Pierre: Like Austen, I will apologize for my English accent. [*audience laughter*] I was appointed Nuncio in Mexico in 2007. I arrived on the 1st of June, and usually when you arrive as a nuncio, some bishops come to greet you at the airport. I was received by a group of bishops, and among them were bishops from the meeting of Aparecida in Brazil. You know the meeting of Aparecida in Brazil? It was three weeks in May. Actually, I had been personally invited to go to Aparecida, but I was coming from Uganda, so I said no, I can't go. The first things I heard from these bishops — and I stayed nine years in Mexico — was their experience of Aparecida. When you come from Africa and you arrive in South America, you have to update yourself about the culture, about what happens, because you live in different worlds. What I heard from these bishops is that they had had a wonderful experience in Aparecida, which was the general meeting of the bishops of South America. During the last century, you have had five big meetings, big assemblies, and they happen every 10 or 15 years. The last one was the fifth such meeting. The third one, which was quite important, happened in 1979 in Puebla. This Aparecida meeting was important because the bishops had reflected upon the situation of the Church in South America. They analyzed the situation as pastors, and then they came together as pastors, and imagined a kind of answer to the situation, a pastoral answer. The result is the so-called document of Aparecida. This document was implemented in the various Churches. Personally, during my nine years in Mexico, I saw the results of Aparecida in the concrete day-to-day pastoral work of the diocese — how it's changed the vision, how it helps the bishops to evangelize in a new context. What struck me at that time — that was 2007 — is that the bishops were speaking about a particular man, and he was called Cardinal Bergoglio, the bishop in Buenos Aires, Argentina. I remember the one who is now the Cardinal Archbishop of Mexico was also one of the main redactors of the final document, and he was telling me how this Cardinal Bergoglio helped the bishops of South America reunite in Aparecida, to look at the reality of the culture, the situation of the countries in this particular time, and helped them also to formulate a response to the challenges of the time. And the document of Aparecida is remarkable for that. This is actually the first document I read when I arrived in Mexico, and I said, "You know, it's something new!" You feel that the pastors, the shepherds, had a real desire to respond to the expectation of the people. The main expectation came for the suffering of all those who have a responsibility to announce the Gospel, to transmit their faith to the new generation, and the difficulty that the parents, the teachers, the priests — everybody — has had in transmitting it. They feel that they are in a new world and new epoch, a new time, and we are actually lost; we don't know what to do, how to do it. I believe that this is something that most of us feel today. In Mexico, for example, you were born a Catholic, and through the family, the school, the parish, you remained a Catholic. But today there is a breakdown in communication, which is not just the normal breakdown between one generation to the other, but it's rather a kind of epochal change coming from the culture, the fragmentation of the culture.

Six years after that meeting in Aparecida, the man who had actually helped the bishops to respond to the needs of the time, to the challenge of the time, became the pope. Some people say, We don't know why they choose that pope. We don't know why, but the Holy Spirit works. There is a Providence of God that works. The mediation of the Church elected Bergoglio to become Pope Francis. They didn't choose an African, they didn't choose a Frenchman — I would have liked that. In the past they chose a Polish man; that was also Providence. Now, however, they chose Bergoglio from South America. The bishops had been looking for responses to the challenge of the time. When Marxism collapsed with the fall of the Berlin wall, a new search was made in the new context, and that was Aparecida. What was the answer? The answer was that in this new situation, we have to provide the people, our people, a Church that helps them in a very concrete way to have a new encounter with Jesus Christ. Because we cannot encounter Jesus if it is not through the Church. But, if the Church doesn't exist, and if it is not a Church that corresponds to the culture, to the desire, to the needs of the people, it will not work. Pope Francis constantly says that: the Church will not work if it does not correspond to what the people need.

So, the effort of the bishops in South America has been precisely to reorient the Church, and in one of the main documents of Aparecida they speak about pastoral conversion. Pastoral conversion means that we have to help the Church to correspond. We cannot live with the Church of yesterday. We cannot live the dream of some people, of some ideology; we need to correspond to the reality of today, because this is the logic of the Incarnation of the Lord. Today, now. *Hic et nunc*. It's interesting to note that the Holy Spirit chose the man who had helped his brother bishops to do that now. Is it not a sign of something that — for me — is a source of wonder? How is it that the document of Aparecida, which was the final instrument of the work of the bishops, was actually given through Pope Francis? Because the problems that had been analyzed by these bishops in Aparecida were actually the problems of the whole world — in different contexts, in different situations, but they remained the same. What Pope Francis did as soon as he was elected was give us his first document, which is still very helpful today. You know it: *Evangelii Gaudium*, the joy of the Gospel. And by the way, *Evangelii Gaudium* is in many ways a copy of the document of Aparecida. Interesting.

Medina: Austen, Archbishop Pierre was talking about how Aparecida becomes a place in which there is a new way of judging modernity. How do you see that, and what is particular about that?

Ivereigh: When I've looked into Aparecida, what amazes me is how well prepared it was. It wasn't just a meeting of bishops, it was the result of a process that took place over many, many, years, that was essentially what we call a synodal process. The local Churches were consulted and they had commissions and research, and basically the question was: Why isn't the Gospel getting through? What are the obstacles to evangelizing today's world? And of course, the answers came back in ways that would be very familiar to us. The transmission belts are broken. The old mechanisms of faith, transmission through culture, through families, through law, are breaking down under the impact of globalization, what we would call now "liquid modernity." It's the same stuff as we all talk about. What I think is different, though, about Aparecida, when I looked at it, was that the Church had undertaken a deep discernment that was not being undertaken by the Church anywhere else in the world. And the discernment question was this: instead of saying, "All this is happening and how terrible it is," or "How sad this is because we're losing what we had and condemning it," what the Church did was discern: they asked, "What is the Holy Spirit asking us to do in this situation?" Firstly, it's asking us to look with the eyes of faith on a wounded and broken world, just like God looks down on the world and sends His Son to save it. You start with the wounds and the needs of humanity. And then the second question is — and this is the question I think the Church was not asking anywhere else — "How does the Church need to change in order to offer the Gospel to these changed and new circumstances?" Instead of lamenting and condemning, the Church discerned and reformed. The call to the Church to change, which is really captured beautifully in *Evangelii Gaudium,* can be summed up in maybe the most famous line in *Evangelii Gaudium,* which is that the Church I dream of, the pope says — I forget the exact quote — becomes a missionary for the sake of the world and not for the sake of her own self-preservation. That, it seems to me, is absolutely the key to the whole Francis project, if I can call it that; which is, essentially, as Archbishop Pierre said, the project of Aparecida. It's there in *Evangelii Guardium.* How do we as a Church need to change in order to offer the Gospel to today's world? Ultimately we start — and I'm in good company when I say this — with the encounter with Christ. We must ask how we as a Church can offer that encounter — *not* how do we keep our institutions going; not how do we ensure we have successful institutions that are powerful and successful and influential; not how do we impose Christianity or maintain Christian values through the law; but, rather, how do we allow people to have the encounter with Christ? And the answer given by Aparecida, and by Pope Francis, was: you go to the margins. It's where the Gospel began. The Gospel always begins, and the evangelization always begins, by going outside the center to the margins, to the places of need. The existential margins, the physical margins, the social margins, and there to encounter God. I think this is the other great insight of Aparecida: rather than saying the Church takes God to people, it says to ask the Church to go out to find God already in the people. This is a great insight and understanding of Latin American theology, which is: God has already visited His people, and if the Church is shrinking, it's because the Church is withdrawing from the people. God isn't leaving the people; God is in the people.

I really understood this in July of last year, when I was in Colegio Maximo in Buenos Aires, which is where Jorge Mario Bergoglio spent a lot of his life. And actually I was in the parish that he helped set up. I was with a group of young people who had just come back from missioning, so they had been on mission for four days, and these young people did exactly what Bergoglio asked his Jesuits to do, which is to go out to people's houses, sit with them, pray with them, listen to them. All sorts of concrete things come out of that. But the really big thing that happened was the effect on *them*, on these young people, because they said, "Wow, these people, they don't come to Church but they have all this experience of God, and they've suffered." One of them said — excuse me if I say it in Spanish, but it sounds really good in Spanish — "Misionando fuimos misionados," which I think you can only translate in English as, "In going out on mission we were missioned too." The point is that the Church and the pope say this in *Evangelii Guardium*: the Church evangelizes itself. Only if we are permanently on mission, offering the encounter and experiencing the encounter, will we be revitalized, will we grow. That, in a sense, is the answer of Aparecida, as re-expressed in *Evangelii Gaudium*, which is at the heart of this pontificate.

Medina: It seems to you as if the provocation that is coming from the pope is not an institutional reform, but a re-discovery of Christianity that is inhabited within the Church.

Pierre: I am convinced that, even in this country, some people have difficulty understanding who Pope Francis is, because where we traveled, some people say a lot about him. Basically, I think it's a lack of understanding. He is our pope, there is no other, there will not be another. I think it's important to know this, because the Church is not a company, it's not a business. Some people think today that the business Church is falling apart. But this is not a business, it's not a company. It's the mystery of God's Presence in the human reality. And we are Church. The work of the Church is to tell people that they are loved by God. But if we in the Church have no contact with the people, if we remain behind our walls, protected, we won't reach the people. And then how could we say to the people they are loved? They will not listen because we are far away. This is what prophecy says: "Go out, tell the people that they are loved by God," and then you will build the Church because the Church is the people of God.

The document of Aparecida, *Evangelii Gaudium*, and all the documents of the pope are saying that. There is a big world today, evangelization, and the Church is for evangelization. This is the key of our understanding. If we don't understand that, we are lost today. The need to evangelize is very urgent today because we are living in a time of change, and people are drifting away from the Church, from us, from the Church institutions. We have to rebuild the Church. This is why he chose the name Francis. "Rebuild my Church."

Ivereigh: I was just going to say I think it does involve some element of institutional reform, because the institution needs to be changed to be adequate to the task it faces. That is what the pope's been doing in Rome these last six years, and it is very important in terms of the changes in the way the finances are managed, in the governance of the Church, and indeed in the whole understanding of the place of the Vatican in relation to the universal Church. There's a lot to be said about all that, but in a way, it's not for its own sake. The Church isn't reformed for its own sake but for the purpose of mission; and insofar as the institution no longer serves the mission, we have to change it; it has to be changed. Not for the purpose of self-preservation, of course. We can recall his now-iconic speech to the Cardinals on the eve of the conclave, which made a deep impact on them and led many of them to believe that he was anointed by the Holy Spirit. He presented an image of the Church, calling it a Church that was basically self-referential, doubled over like the paralyzed woman in the Luke, incapable of looking out but rather focused in on herself, living from its own light and not from the light of Christ. It was a devastating critique, absolutely devastating. And he said the Church is called to live the joy of evangelizing, and not to exist for itself. What is the Church for? It's the ultimate purpose question. Certainly the media treat us as if we are a corporation only interested in ourselves, in looking good, in covering up our dirty secrets because we exist for us. In other words, it's interesting that the perception of the modern world is that the Church exists for itself, not for the sake of humanity. We have to be broken, in a sense, so that people can see that the Church is there to serve humanity, to heal the wounds of humanity, and not to exist for itself.

Medina: You have had the opportunity to meet also with the Pope, and this correction that Austen Ivereigh is talking about, not being self-referential, is something that the pope mentioned to you when you met him with the Movement, with Communion and Liberation, in Saint Peter's Square. You lead a Movement in the Church that is not an institution. How do you see the pope actually leading or helping you in the work that you do?

Fr. Julián Carrón: I think that's one of the most important issues in the way the pope is leading the Church. The Church has a problem with modernity in the world. In this particular moment, the most important value for the modern world is freedom. So the question is, How can this be offered? How can we offer an answer to their freedom? I think the pope incarnates very well the phrase of a poet, Péguy: "We are the first generation after Christ without Christ." Therefore, the only possibility of addressing this situation is through the announcement of the Christian event as it was announced for the first time, 2000 years ago. Because people need other people. And only if I can encounter somebody who incarnates — today, in the modern world — a way of dealing with reality in such an attractive way, can I be helped in the fight against nihilism, against nothingness, against the lack of hope, the lack of meaning. The crisis we are dealing with is an occasion to understand what Christianity is. Most people have not been reached by the Church, by the Gospel. They don't know anything about it. Or what they know is something not interesting to them. Von Balthasar, in the last century, said that this kind of reasoning was not convincing anybody; it had lost the power to convince because Christianity is not a speech, Christianity is not a set of rules, Christianity is not a doctrine. Christianity is an *event*. It is crucial in our dealing with the crisis to recognize the nature of Christianity, because without this, it will be impossible for Christianity to be conveyed to others. And this is the challenge for all of us Christians, not the Church, all of us: that we meet everybody. In a job, in the neighborhood, during our free time, on a vacation, everywhere: in every place we meet people. We must offer to the other our way of being in reality — not outside the reality, not just this Sunday morning at Church — but in reality, in our way of dealing with the news, in our way of dealing with the crisis, with the lack of hope, with the lack of meaning. The Church has an institutional aspect, of course, and we cannot deny it. But at the same time, the Church reaches people through the members of the Church, through the Body of Christ. That means our life, our witnesses, our way of being human beings. And for this reason, the only possibility of conveying Christianity is to become witnesses to the newness of Christianity. This is the challenge. It is useless to keep discussing about grouping the Church for or against the pope. Useless. Because this doesn't make a new Christian. The blog against the pope doesn't reawaken the faith in anybody. How can we become Christians? This is the real question for us. If we look at the beginning, the first two disciples who met Christ were attracted by something that is not today readily accepted: authority. Authority is somebody who makes me grow in my humanity. Only when they met Christ and became so struck by his humanity did they decide to follow Him. They didn't want to lose what they were seeing before them. Only by becoming disciples, followers, could they recognize and become familiar with His humanity. For this reason, the problem is not an institution. The problem is: Where are the people who can convey this kind of Christianity? Because many of the reformation programs are taking for granted that there is a human being who is shaped in such a way by Christianity. But many times *we* are the first one who need to be evangelized.

The pope is this giant that the Lord has given to us to reawaken, to recreate in us a possibility of living Christianity with joy, with the possibility of encountering anybody, whatever his ideology, his religion. I can meet whomever, in whatever situation, in whatever religion, in whatever circumstances, in whatever ideology, because I am not afraid of their freedom. The pope went to Abu Dhabi and to Egypt, and to some of the most challenging places in the world, as a Christian. This is our challenge, today for all of us. We are worried about a reformation of the Church when we should instead be worried about a reformation of ourselves, because that is the only real answer to the problem. When we arrive every day to our job, our colleagues don't care about all the questions of the Church; rather, they need to meet somebody in whom they recognize something so attractive that it challenges their freedom. This is what happened in the Gospel: John and Andrew met Jesus for only two hours, but the following day they were desiring to look for Him. Christianity — this is the most important truth that the pope is conveying to the Church — can only be conveyed by attraction, by the power of attraction, because the power of beauty is unarmed. Only if we can convey this beauty will there be a chance for Christianity today.

Medina: The pope, in his first encyclical, says to be joyful, be a witness. But this kind of witness, it seems to me, is not the witness of a strong-willed, well-behaved person, but is the witness of a changed man. After listening to Father Carrón, I recall now many of the things that Austen said before. A simple man who presents himself as a simple man, but yet is extraordinary. Is this what the pope is asking of us?

Pierre: Father Carrón, you insist that our faith is based on an encounter — and this is the Gospel, by the way. Our tendency is to transform it into ideas and ideologies, because we all need the security of ideas and ideologies. But that is not our faith. My security exists when I follow Jesus; that's it, that's my only security. I have faith in Him, and I believe in Him, and He will lead me where He wants. There is always a danger in the Church and in our institutions to think that we need ideas, ideologies, to be secure. Does it mean that we don't need an institution? Institutions are necessary because this is, actually, the incarnation: it is the incarnation of the process of salvation in the world. We therefore need the Church. We cannot eliminate the Church. I have heard some people lately saying, "I don't believe in the Church anymore, I don't believe in the bishops because they're…I don't believe in the priests, I just believe in Jesus." But that is a heresy: you can believe in Jesus only if you believe in the Church. This is why I think Pope Francis a marvelous guide for the Church. A guide tells you what you need to do and what you need to avoid. What you have to do is to follow Jesus. To be disciples is to live the beatitudes, to listen to the Word of God, and to follow Him day after day. And what to avoid is precisely not to create another god, another master, the only one is Jesus. Some priests and bishops are not happy with Pope Francis, because they say, "The pope is always criticizing us and we are not so bad." Of *course* you are not so bad. The pope does not say that you are bad; the pope asks you to be what you are supposed to be. But he says the same thing to lay people, because he wants the Church, as Father Carrón says, and I think this is also a key word — to be a response to the change of time, in the new time, the world witness. The witness who is attractive. If I invite people to my house but charge a fee to be evangelized, people will not come. You are not evangelized if you pay the fee; you are evangelized when you meet somebody who is a witness of Jesus.

This is our vocation and the mission for all of us. We are all missionary disciples. What is a missionary disciple? Well, it comes from Aparecida again. I think it's interesting to know that. Aparecida said that in this new time, when it's not so easy to transmit the faith from one generation to the other, to announce the Gospel, we need to create a new institution that is attractive, and that helps people to have a new encounter with Jesus and therefore become disciples. The purpose of the Church is to make disciples. This is what Jesus said to His first friends: "Make disciples all over the world! Go!" The Church is not a club of Jesus' friends, and the pope is not the CEO of a big business. Whatever you do, it is to become disciples. Then, a disciple necessarily will make other disciples, will become a missionary. But being missionaries does not necessarily mean we all need to go to Africa. This is the vocation of certain missionaries, of course, but as Father Carrón said, your family is the first place you need to be a missionary. In school, in business, with friends — there is an urgency for a missionary Church today.

Medina: There are two words that continually appear: the words *authority* and *freedom*. And I notice that you are basically saying that Pope Francis is taking the Church through the Spiritual Exercises, through a journey of discernment. And he's the authority. I was struck by your answer to my initial question, about what Pope Francis is like in person: "I felt free in front of him." So there's a connection between authority and freedom.

Ivereigh: Pope Francis is a master of spiritual discernment, truly a master of the Spiritual Exercises of Saint Ignatius. He spent his life giving them to people, and he understands the Spiritual Exercises as a manual for understanding the motions of the Spirit. How does the Holy Spirit act within us? And conversely, what about the bad spirit that is always trying to obstruct the good Spirit speaking to us? How does the bad spirit work? That's really the art of discernment. Freedom comes from embracing, being open to the Holy Spirit. Receptivity. His authority as a spiritual guide is simply his experience of how this works. H has — and all the Jesuits in Argentina will tell you this — an extraordinary capacity for detecting the deceits of the bad spirit. There's a paradox about him, actually, because I described him in *The Great Reformer* as a combination of Machiavellian and desert Saint. He has the innocence of the dove but the cunning of serpents, and that's what Jesus invited us to have. He has an incredibly pure heart and innocence about him, but he has an extraordinary capacity to detect cunning. He's got a cunning astuteness that makes him a brilliant leader. But what is he doing right now with the Church, in this crisis we're living through? He's leading the Church through the Spiritual Exercises. He sees this crisis, this tribulation, as an opportunity for conversion. In desolation there is always a grace. God is always offering us a grace, a chance, an opportunity for conversion, and we're invited to take it. If I had longer, I would explain where I think the pope sees the conversion taking place in the tribulation of right now. But without going there, I will just say that I trust him as the spiritual director of an institution often in desolation, often experiencing tribulation, but which also has the possibility of converting. There is a grace here. We will be better on the other side. It's like our own journey of conversion: it consists of putting Christ at the center, following Christ rather than the things that we often claim are good and very religious, but are basically idols. I was very touched by what Father Carrón said. If there is something that unites the modern

Church and the modern papacies, it is Giussani's great observation about Christianity as an encounter. Pope Benedict says in *Deus Caritas Est* that Christianity does not begin with a lofty idea or an ethical proposition, but with the encounter with a person who changes your horizon. Where does it next appear? Aparecida. Pope Benedict's observation opens the Aparecida document. Aparecida put it right up front. In *Evangelii Guardium* it appears very early on. Francis quotes it and says, "This is the heart of the Gospel." This is the *filo rosso*, as you say in Italian, this is the golden thread that unites the modern papacies. Benedict saw it very, very, clearly, and Francis is really acting on it. The Church went wrong at some point. It closed in on itself. It turned Christianity into a precept and an idea, when in fact it's an encounter. Therefore, the journey of conversion is to put Christ back at the center so we can become missionary disciples, people who have experienced that encounter, and who are then able to offer it to a confused and hurting world.

Medina: I want to close with a question to you, Father Carrón, that is very similar to what I asked Austen. Something that I've noticed while traveling around the United States, is that in the places where the culture is more secularized, and therefore the impact of a conception of freedom as "do what you please" is most clear, there is a natural reaction on the part of Christians to retreat into a more rigid stance, something that doesn't move. It feels as if there is almost a contradiction between authority as something safe and secure, and freedom as something unsafe and uncertain, where everything is fluid. In our conversation today, the three of you have talked about authority and freedom as feeding off of each other. You began by saying that the test of time is a test of freedom. That if Christianity is true today, it should be capable of answering the need of the person's freedom. And like I said, I was struck by Austen's reaction in front of a Christian, that he felt free. If you could just say a few words about this, because the Christian conception of freedom and authority seems so unusual. We usually understand freedom as "doing whatever we want," and authority as, "You have to do what I tell you." It feels as though we're talking about two different things, two different conceptions of authority and freedom.

Carrón: This is the test of our relationship with the modern world, because in front of chaos the only solution appears to be some kind of rigid recovering of Christianity. But that's not it. Every conception on the crisis, every concrete gesture of Christianity can be verified in history. The Word became Man. Speech became incarnated in a human being — this is Christianity. He shows that there is a way of conveying this particular conception of life, this proposal for living, that can be incarnated in somebody. We can see that many peole are so afraid of the reality that they want a shelter to protect them from the risks coming from outside the Church. But the Church didn't have any fear at the beginning, when it began in a multi-cultural society, the Roman Empire. This was seen instead as the opportunity to convey the newness of Christianity in such a powerful way. So, we are at the beginning again. We live in a multi-cultural society in which everybody chooses to do whatever they want, and this means we must have something more attractive to answer the crucial desire for fulfillment that every human being carries in his own heart. This challenge is not only for the Church, but as the proposal to answer the crisis of today, because the crisis is not only the problem of the Church, it is the problem of the schools, it is the problem of education, it is a problem of society, it is a problem of meaning, it is a problem of hope, it is a problem of fear. This is an interesting moment for the Church. The real, original nature of Christianity can be interesting for most of the people that we have in mind. But there is a condition: Christianity must be Christianity. Because many of the ways in which we convey Christianity are only a reduction of Christianity to a speech, to another thing, to a set of rules, to our feelings. The Christianity that John and Andrew met was not reduced to any of those things. It was not something imposed by power, not something forced.

Pierre: It's true that freedom is the big challenge of our time. However, when we speak about freedom we must also speak about the education of freedom. You said that the pope is like a spiritual director for humanity. A spiritual director is somebody who accompanies a person to use his or her freedom in the right way. The problem with the modernity is that people quite often have disconnected freedom from the concept of responsibility. Pope Francis is really the pope of modernity. Recall his famous statement, "Who am I to judge?" This was him putting himself as a pope in front of the concept of modernity: "I respect your freedom." He is the pope of a Church that has placed at the center of its action the concept of education.

What is the role of the family? Education. What is the role of the Church? Education. What is the role of the state? Education. To educate people so they may use their humanity for the good of themselves and others. This concept of education is so important. By the way, there is a famous book by Giussani, *The Risk of Education*. When we as a Church take the risk of educating, it means that we also are ready to take the risk of freedom. This is why the work of the Church is so challenging. We don't impose a theory, a doctrine; we take the risk of educating people to become disciples of Jesus. If we don't do this work, taking seriously this part of education, we are failing as a Church.

Medina: Thank you very much, Archbishop Pierre, Austen Ivereigh, and Father Julián Carrón. [*audience applause*]

Something
TO START FROM
February 15–17, 2019
Metropolitan Pavilion, 125 W. 18th St., NYC
ÖBERG
ROBBERTO
LUNINE

Origins of Life and
Existence of Extraterrestrial

Beyond the Moon...to the Farthest Reaches

*The search for planets outside our solar system. With **Jonathan Lunine**, Director, Cornell Center for Astrophysics and Planetary Science; **Karin Öberg**, Professor of Astronomy, Harvard University; and moderated by **Massimo Robberto**, AURA Observatory Scientist at the Space Telescope Science Institute*

Introduction

Researching the unknown is one of the deepest aspects of the human heart. Also, when there have been no immediate advantages, the need for exploring the world, and new worlds, has always been alive, boosted by a secret attraction for reality. Our innate need for novelty represents a continuous prompt to "go beyond," to be open to meeting the unexpected, the unknown, hoping that what we may discover will tell us something about our presence in the world, our origins, our destiny. Our ancestral need for meeting the Mystery, expressed in the art and literature of all cultures, did not only bring to a great expansion our knowledge of the world, but to a deeper awareness of ourselves as well. For centuries we explored our planet. Then, we began exploring our solar system, and 50 years ago we landed on the moon. Today we are on the threshold of a new, radical expansion of the matter. In recent years, the presence of a huge number of planets that revolve around other stars, the so-called "extrasolar planets," or "exoplanets," has been revealed. They are very distant worlds and even the closest, at the moment, is completely beyond the reach of our spaceships.

But some of them may have characteristics that can accommodate life. Is it possible? What do we know about these planets today? How are they formed? Under what conditions can earth-like environments be created elsewhere? And if indeed some distant planet houses life, what life could it be? Finally, why is it that we are passionate and worried about the idea that elsewhere, somewhere far away, there can be life?

❖   ❖   ❖   ❖   ❖

Massimo Robberto: Good evening. I'm Massimo Robberto, and I have the pleasure and the honor of moderating, guiding us through this fascinating encounter with two protagonists, two absolute superstars of contemporary astrophysical research. As I was preparing this meeting, I thought of myself fifty years ago. I was at the age when you climb trees. You climb trees because they are there. You climb the tree because you can reach farther out and climb higher and higher and you reach the last branches. And then, on one evening, we discovered that beyond the last branch there is the moon. The moon is within reach; they were landing on the moon. And for people my age, and the age of Jonathan, I would say that was a life-changing experience. We realized how powerful is the attraction of reality, the provocation of reality, something that called us to go beyond, to go farther, to climb the highest mountain, because it's there and because at the end you learned something about yourself. All the great climbers and explorers will tell you, "I did it for myself," because we want to know how far we can go, trying to affirm "something" that calls us.

And today this is clearly expressed in a most powerful way through scientific research. Science is done exactly for this reason: reality is there, it attracts us, and we want to know, we want to explore, we would like to even go there. And at the forefront of scientific research in these days, probably the hottest area of contemporary astrophysics is the discovery of planets around other stars. We are discovering a treasure trove of worlds, and we wonder if we are alone in the universe, if there are other places where we can live. It is more and more real than it has ever been. In the past it was a philosophical question. Well, now is starts to be a scientific question. So, to know where we are and to see the implication for our awareness of ourselves, we have invited Jonathan Lunine and Karin Öberg. I must say their biographies are so long that I simply invite you to take the program and go through it, because it will take forever to read it to you. But do let me say a few words to frame who we have here at the table this evening.

Jonathan is David C. Duncan Professor in Physical Science and the Director of the Center for Astrophysics and Planetary Science at Cornell, so basically he's the boss of Cornell University, one of the historic centers of astrophysics in the United States. He is interested in how planets form, evolve; what processes maintain and establish habitability; the possibility of finding life, and what kind of environments may host the chemistry sophisticated enough to support life. Jonathan is a protagonist in the exploration of the solar system. He worked on the radar and other instruments on the Cassini probe that went to Saturn. He is co-investigator in the Juno mission, and in the next few years will probe one of the most fascinating bodies of the solar system, Europa. He is also, I must say, interdisciplinary scientist for the James Webb Space Telescope, so in some sense, is *my* boss — I answer to this guy. He is a member, of course, of several academies, starting with the National Academy of Science; is chair of several NASA National Science Foundation boards; strategic planning committees from NASA, etc. — read the biography. I think this is enough.

Karin is more scary, because Karin was a baby genius, and like me she was Champion of Sweden of Chemistry. She went to the Olympics in Chemistry, and immediately at the end of high school she went to Caltech, as you know, the number one university in the region. So: Sweden, then Caltech, and after Caltech there is really no other place in the world to go except Harvard, so she went to Harvard. She had a little detour for one year at the University of Virginia, but Harvard immediately captured her and she's now a professor at Harvard: Professor of Astrophysics. Karin is interested in a fascinating discipline, Astrochemistry, which is basically the chemical processes as they appear around the universe, and the end of this chemical processes is most fascinating, as she will tell us. I think I've talked too much; it's time to listen to them. Jonathan.

Jonathan Lunine: Thank you, Massimo. One of the most profound questions that we can ask as human beings is in what way are we special? Are we alone in the cosmos? From the spiritual point of view, we understand how we are special. From the scientific point of view, the question really is whether there might be other kinds of life elsewhere in the cosmos, intelligent life, and the first step in understanding that is to know how many planets there are elsewhere in the cosmos. This is a question that has fascinated people for centuries. If you go back 800 years, you find that St. Albert the Great — in the 1200s! — asked the question, "Is there only one world?" Do there exist many worlds or but a single world? This is one of the most noble and exalted questions in the study of nature. Now, he decided on the side of one world, but he also had a lot of great insights about the universe. He thought the Milky Way galaxy, for example, was made of stars long before the telescope was invented. And then we go on to the 1300s and encounter Dante and *The Divine Comedy*. If you read the very last line of *The Divine Comedy*, it talks about the love that moves the sun and the other stars, and so already there was a realization within the European framework that the sun was one of many stars. But it wasn't until Copernicus and the publication of his book and his model — which proved that the earth, in fact, was not the center of the cosmos, but instead revolves around the sun as did the other planets — that people began thinking about the question of how many other planets there might be.

In the late 1500s, Giordano Bruno, who was not a scientist but rather a philosopher, thought about this and wrote about it — in Italian, of course. He said there must be countless worlds. If there are countless suns in the heavens, then there must be countless planets all rotating around their suns, and in exactly the same way as the seven planets of our solar system. But then he went on to say something very important and very profound, given the fact that he wasn't a scientist and the telescope was just being invented. He asked the question, Why don't we see these other planets? Why are they invisible? And he answered his own question by saying that we see the suns, the stars, because they're self-luminous; they're very bright. But we don't see the planets because they are simply too dim; they are lost in the glare of their parent stars. And that statement was exactly correct. In fact, if you look below the statue of Giordano Bruno, there's a modern image of a star as seen through a telescope on the earth. The light of the star has actually been blocked out by a disk called a coronagraph, and even though the light has been blocked out some light escapes. It escapes around the edge of the disc. It's distorted by the earth's atmosphere, by the optics of the telescope, and so if you want to see a planet at the position of the earth around that star, you have to look most of the way into the center where the glare is. It would be impossible to see the earth. The planet that you do see, which is indicated by the arrow, is very far from that star. It's the equivalent of being out at the edge or beyond the edge of our solar system.

This was recognized back in the late 1500s, early 1600s, but interestingly enough, as modern astronomy progressed, the question of whether there might be other planets began to be less interesting in the 1800s and 1900s — partly because it turned out to be very difficult to actually *find* these planets. How do you pull them out from under the glare of their parent stars? Here's an old textbook I used as a freshman taking astronomy back in 1976: *Introductory Astronomy and Astrophysics*. There are three chapters in this book on the solar system, and not a single mention anywhere else about planets around other stars. Nothing at all. The field became kind of quiet for a long time, but eventually began to blossom again because astronomers found ways to use tricks, essentially, to find planets around other stars. After more than a decade of efforts with these techniques, planets began to be found. So now the field of what's called exoplanets — planets around other stars — is one of the most popular and exciting branches of astronomy. There are textbooks written and popular books written. This is a textbook called *Exoplanets*, edited by Sara Seager, a prominent exoplanet astronomer at MIT. If you go to websites like **exoplanet.eu**, you'll find that every day the number of planets is increasing. The number of discovered planets — I just pulled this off the web — is 3,975 in 2,970 planetary systems. And some of those systems have multiple planets — 653 of them.

And what astronomers have found is that, on average, for every star in the Milky Way galaxy there is a planet. Now, we haven't looked at every star in the Milky Way galaxy for planets, this is extrapolating from discoveries made closer to our own solar system, but the statistics are pretty good. On average there is one planet for every star in the Milky Way, which means there are perhaps 200 billion planets in our galaxy. Now how do we actually detect these planets? How have these things been detected? I want to spend a good part of my time on this question, because I think it's important to show how astronomers use physics to tease out the signature of a planet from underneath the glare of the star. In this lovely animation that was prepared by the Planetary Habitability Lab at the University of Puerto Rico in Arecibo, you see five different ways to detect planets, and in all but one of those cases, you're actually not looking directly at the planet, you're looking at either the effect of the planet on its parent star, or you're looking indirectly at the effect of the planet on the signature of another star behind it, which I'll describe in a minute.

Yes, this is an astronomy lesson, and yes, there will be a quiz afterwards. Let's start out with that panel on the upper left, that animation, and what that animation shows is a planet and a star. Now notice that the planet is not actually orbiting around a fixed star, which is the way we think of things when we think of our solar system. Both the planet and the star are orbiting around their common center of mass. So, if these two objects were equal in mass, if they were two equal mass stars, they would actually be orbiting around a center that's exactly halfway between them. But, because the planet is much less massive than the star, the planet makes a big orbit and the star makes a little orbit around that center of mass, which is shown by the red cross in the diagram. Now imagine also that that planet is invisible. You're the observer on the earth; you really cannot see that planet. It is lost in the glare of the parent star. So how can you find the effect of that planet? Well, one way — which was the way that astronomers in the 1960s thought would be the only way to do it — is shown in the box below. It's called astrometry. Look at the animation of that star wobbling around its center of mass, the system; imagine it's a point — the way that stars look in the night sky; you would see that point of light making a small circle relative to the fixed background of stars. That's all that astrometry is. It's observing the cyclical or periodic motion of a star caused by a companion. Very simple technique, and the little box is attempting to depict that. By the way, those numbers underneath each box are the number of planets discovered by each technique. The slide is by now a bit old, so each of those techniques has discovered between two and three times more planets. Okay, so that's astrometry.

It turns out it has been very difficult to make astrometry work for various reasons, so another approach, the one that really broke the field open, is shown on the upper row in the middle. It's called "radial velocity." Now, you see the star in that little panel there becoming red and blue, and then red and then blue again. So what's happening? To understand what's happening, you have to imagine taking that image of the star, and turning the whole thing 90 degrees so that it's facing you, or even better, I'm going to be the star. Actually I *am* the star, because I have the stage right now. [*audience laughter*] I'm going to be *this* star, and I'm going to make my little orbits, okay? And you are the observers. So, here I go. I'm making my circle. Now for part of the circle, I'm moving side to side from your point of view, but at other times I'm moving towards you, and I'm moving away from you. Now, when I'm moving towards you, the light that I'm emitting — because a star is a self-luminous object — the wavelength of that light, the color of that light, gets shortened by the motion, my motion as a star. So, if the wavelength gets shorter, I'm going to appear bluer. When I'm moving away and emitting light toward you, the wavelength is being stretched out, and so now I look red.

Just by this motion, this radial motion back and forth as part of the small circle, I'm turning blue and then red and then blue and then red. The problem is this: the change in color is so subtle that you really can't see it, and so what astronomers have had to do is use a time-honored technique called spectroscopy, where you spread out the light from the star using a prism, or actually today we use something called a grading. You can see the individual wavelengths of light, and in that spectrum from the star there are dark lines, cut outs, where atoms in the atmosphere of that star, at well-determined wavelengths, are absorbing the light. Those are fiducial lines in the spectrum of the star. Now, as the star moves toward you, those lines are going to shift toward the blue; thus shorter wavelengths. As the star is moving away, they're going to shift to the red, longer wavelengths, and astronomers learned how to observe this very, very, precisely in the 1980s and 1990s, and that broke open the field of exoplanets. Radial velocity was the first technique to really detect a lot of planets.

Another technique: "transit," which is in the upper right. A little simpler. I'm going to be the star again, and this little clicker is going to be the planet. It happens that the orbit of the planet, the plane of that orbit is nicely aligned to you. Most of the time that doesn't happen, but occasionally it does. So, as the planet is sweeping around in front of me, it's partly blocking my light. Okay, here I am a luminous object, and this unilluminated planet is blocking part of the light. As you can see in that depiction, the light of the star dims as the planet passes in front of it, and it does so in a very regular, periodic way during each orbit of the planet. Now, in order to detect these transits, you have to be able to measure the brightness of the star very, very, well. It's a drop of about one percent for a planet the size of Jupiter, and about a 100th of a percent for a planet the size of the earth. The best way to do this is to go into space, so NASA's Kepler mission became the king of planet discoveries by using the transit technique to discover more than 3,000 planetary candidates.

Okay, the last two techniques. One is called microlensing, which is very exotic and depends upon general relativity. What Einstein realized was that massive objects bend light, distort the path of light through space. A star is a massive object. Imagine a situation where you have a background star in the distance, and because stars in our galaxy have some random motion, foreground stars will occasionally pass in front of the background. You can't see that with your eye, but it can be measured by telescopes. So, when that foreground star passes in front of the background star, the light from the background star gets bent by the gravity of the foreground star. Bent in such a way that it's very much like a convex lens, and the starlight, the background star, will temporarily brighten as you see in that panel on the bottom center. But if you look at that panel, you'll notice that after the slow brightening and dimming there's a sudden pulse. And that sudden pulse happens if the foreground star, the lens star, has a planet orbiting around it in just about the right position to re-magnify the image of the background star. You can think of that planet as a kind of distortion on the lens that represents the foreground star. If the planet is in the right place, there will be a second, sudden brightening, and boom, you have a planet. That's a tough technique to use. It requires staring into space at a large number of stars. Not very many planets have been detected that way, but it's an interesting technique.

And then, finally, direct imaging, which is a technique of trying to block the light of the parent star so that you can bring out the faint light of a planet. There's a lot of work being done to make that technique sensitive enough, by going into space to be able to actually see another earth out from under the light of the parent star.

These are some of the tools that are used on the ground, in observatories, and in space. You see Kepler at the bottom right, and a new telescope, the Transiting Exoplanet Survey Satellite, just launched last year, picking up from Kepler. I want to focus on one really interesting system called the TRAPPIST-1 system. The name of that planetary system, the first one to be discovered by this particular group in Europe, does pay homage to the Trappist order of monks; not to their religious devotion, but to the beer that they apparently produce and that these astronomers drink [*audience laughter*]. Indeed, that's the case. That's why they named it. So, the TRAPPIST-1 system is one of the most interesting systems, because it has seven planets orbiting around the star, and those seven planets are in really tight orbits around that star. In fact, the farthest one is closer to its star than Mercury is to the sun, so it's a very compact system. And furthermore, the star itself is a small star. If you look in the lower right on the slide, you'll see a little piece of the sun. And scaled to the same scale, is the size of that TRAPPIST-1 star, which is quite a bit smaller than our sun. In fact, it's really not much bigger than the planet Jupiter. The planets of that system are about the size of Earth, down to about the size of Mars, so they are considerably larger than the moons of Jupiter, which one might have thought would be a fair comparison. There are these seven planets roughly the size of Earth or Mars, orbiting around this star, and we'd like to know: Are any of them habitable? Can they support life? What we really want to know is: Are they so close to their parent star that the water would boil off? Are they so far away that the water would freeze like on Mars, or is it just right? It turns out that you can do a calculation. You can lay out these seven planets on a graph according to the amount of light that they get from this small red star that is their parent star. And it turns out that if we take the earth, and we say that the amount of light that the earth gets is equal to one, that one of those planets gets the same amount of light from its parent star that the earth gets from our sun — and that might be the habitable planet in the TRAPPIST-1 system.

So how did these planets form? If there's so many planets in the galaxy, what is the process by which these planets are created? And the answer seems to be a very old one that goes back to Laplace and Descartes, which is that planetary systems form in disks, spun out as the gas and dust that will become the central star collapses from a much larger — maybe something a light year across — down to something the size of our solar system. It turns out that all of this material, this nascent material in the galaxy from which stars form, has a little bit of rotation to it. As it collapses — just like an ice skater when she pulls in her arms as she's spinning faster — as this material gets more compact it spins faster, eventually spinning so fast that the centrifugal force pushes material out in the form of a disk. Now, in the 1950s and '60s, astronomers didn't believe this because they couldn't figure out how to get the mass from the disk, the matter from the disk, into the star and leave the rotational momentum out in the disk itself. But astronomical observations showed that disks are very, very, common. And this is a beautiful, very recent image of a disk of the HL Tau System from the ALMA radio telescope system in the Atacama Desert in South America. You not only see a disk, but you can see cleared lanes in that disk; probably the result of planet formation happening: early planets, having just formed, cleared a lane of dust and gas out from the disk.

Astronomers, as far as they can tell, find that many stars, perhaps most stars, spin out disks as they're forming, and that's why planets are so common. But how do you get from the dust to the planets themselves? Well, we're learning about that in our own solar system. The New Horizons spacecraft, which visited Pluto a few years ago, just passed the most distant object ever investigated directly by humanity. It's an object called Ultima Thule, well beyond the orbits of the giant planets, out about forty times or more the distance of the earth from the sun, and it's kind of a museum piece that shows us that smaller bodies stick together and grow into bigger bodies. Here are two pieces that have stuck together to something about 20 miles across, and if the process had continued, there would have been growth to bigger and bigger things. We can simulate that growth in a computer.

I'm going to show you very quickly a simulation done by myself and two colleagues, where we start out with material about the size of the moon, and we use the gravity of Jupiter to stir that material up and make larger bodies. We start out with this material: the reddest is closer to the sun, the bluest is farther from the sun. As time goes on, the planets closer to the sun are going to grow to be bigger — but notice they're going to change color, because they're getting material scattered by the gravity of Jupiter, which contains a lot of water that's going to be added to their mass as they grow. It's quite possible that in our own solar system the presence of Jupiter was important in delivering the water we need for life, and organic molecules which we also need for life.

Hundreds of billions of stars in our Milky Way galaxy, hundreds of billions of planets in our Milky Way galaxy, and in the cosmos at large there are hundreds of billions of galaxies. I'm not going to try to multiply those numbers together, you can do it yourself, but it's a lot of planets. The question then arises: Might there be life on these planets? You'll hear more about that from Professor Öberg in a minute, but I want to close by emphasizing that all of these techniques depend upon our confidence that the laws we can determine in the laboratory on Earth are operating across vast cosmic distances. And the assumption that the laws of nature are immutable and reliable and constant comes not from science itself but from the Western tradition, it comes from the Judeo-Christian tradition of understanding our universe as the creation of an omnipotent God who has made for us a place that is regular and predictable, and which we can, therefore, study. This comes from both biblical and traditional sources. For example, I quote here from the *Letter of St. Clement to the Corinthians*, where he says "The sun and moon, with the companies of the stars, roll on in harmony according to His command. The unsearchable places of abysses, and the indescribable arrangements of the lower world, are restrained by the same laws." And so, long before Galileo trained his telescope on the heavens, it was realized that this universe, this created universe with its regularity, was there for us to study as a kind of a grace, as a kind of a gift, and in doing so we're learning marvelous things about our place in it. Thank you. [*audience applause*]

Karin Öberg: It is a true pleasure to be here. Thank you so much for coming. I will just move on directly from where Jonathan, Professor Lunine, ended, and talk about how we try to figure out the probability that there is life on other planets, and how we think life originated here on Earth.

We live in an era where we know that stars are not just cold stars; they're worlds with their own planetary systems, and that's going to be where we spend most of our time: thinking about life in these systems. But before going there, I want to spend a couple of minutes just thinking about the importance of astronomy in general, of understanding our cosmos in general, for having a relationship with God and understanding God as a creator. If we go back to the religions that were in the Middle East before God revealed Himself to Israel, what people would see when they looked up at the skies would be something like this. [*shows slide*] The skies were alive with gods and demi-gods vying for their favors, providing blessings and curses. What the Hebrews did to this cosmos was incredibly dramatic. They killed off the gods; they killed off the gods for a creation that had been spoken into existence, that was peaceful, that was good. Instead of a god of the sun and a god of the moon, you had two lamps. The Hebrews' understanding of their God certainly informed their cosmology, but it was also things about the cosmology that must have formed their understanding of God. If you look at the physics of this cosmology, it's a vault, it's a flat Earth, there's an underworld. This is a contained cosmos in which it's quite easy to imagine where God is: He is outside of this cosmos. This cosmology was replaced by the time that we arrive at the early Christian Church, with a cosmology coming out of the Greek world, which incorporated both new data and new physics. The new data was that the earth is round, which had been known for a long time. The new physics were the Aristotelean physics, which takes *teleos* very seriously, that things are moving towards where they are meant to be.

This cosmology, too, must have informed the early Christians' view of their creator God. This cosmos is incredibly well-ordered, where things are moving in the right directions — an icon of the ordering within the Creator Himself. But this cosmology, too, was replaced for the Church in quite dramatic forms. The heliocentric cosmos came into being in the 16th and 17th centuries. In itself, the moving of the center of the cosmos from the earth to the sun might not seem like a very big change, but when combined with the mechanistic physics that developed at the same time, we get a very different cosmology: a clockwork cosmology. And God becomes a mathematician who created this perfect cosmos, wound it up like a clock, and then let it run. Such a cosmos doesn't really need a God to sustain it in the same obvious way as the earlier cosmologies did. This cosmology continued to develop into the 19th century, mainly becoming bigger and — for metaphysical reasons — eternal. We don't want to put limits on God. He could have created an eternal universe if he had wanted, but there are some difficulties intuiting how to fit the creation in Genesis with an eternal and infinite cosmos. If you live in a cosmos that's always been there, then you don't really have to ask the question of when was it created or who created it. So maybe it's not so strange that, by the turn of the 20th century, you find that a lot of physicists are atheists. Not all, of course, for we have some very famous Catholic scientists from that era. But many are now atheistic. Then, something happened. Starting in the 19th century and developing into the 20th century, looking at astronomy through a combination of Einstein's equations and the genius of Fr. Lemat, we realize that we don't live in a universe that's static. We live in a universe that is developing over time, that's emerging from something very small and very simple into something very big and very complex. We see it in cosmology. We see it when we look at individual stars and planets, which not only have a beginning, they have an end. Every year, seven new stars form in our galaxy and a few stars go out of existence. This, too, should change how we view God as the creator. We still have God the mathematician — I mean, they still believe that this is a world guided by physical loss on all scales. But if we look at this emerging world, we also see God the artist. He's still in the middle of creating His masterpiece. And of course, we know through revelation that He then does this incredible, scandalous thing: He steps into His creation to save it. But more about that later.

This is God the artist, this is the God who just enjoys seeing things developing and giving this ridiculous dignity to His creatures, who are going to be co-creators of their own destiny. Now what I would claim with Professor Ninez is that, with the coming of exoplanets, we have once again changed the cosmology that we live in. The question is: What does this tell us about the creator? Well, I think it mostly just reinforces what we already were learning during the 19th and 20th centuries, that this is a God who enjoys a variety of created things. But this of course leaves a question: If we have all these planets around other stars that are worlds in their own right, how many of them are living worlds? Will we one day encounter extraterrestrial life? How would that affect our theology and our understanding of God and our relationship with Him?

What is the probability that there is life out there? A natural place to start is with the one planet we know has life, which is Earth. Now, on Earth, we can trace back the origins of life by looking at the pattern, the genetic pattern in living and extinct life forms. When we do that, we find we can trace all life on Earth back to a lost common ancestor that lived somewhere around three to three-and-a-half billion years ago. This is probably not the first life that emerged on Earth, but it is an early, early life form. And up here to the right you see Darwin's first attempt at this tree of life. How did this first life happen? We don't know for sure. We think that the following scenario is reasonable. If you go back to the very early Earth, right after it formed, we had a moon impact and things cooled down a bit. We're now around four billion years ago. We had water, we had chemicals combined into more and more complex molecules, and this prebiotic scheme, these more complex molecules then combined into forming RNA, which is very similar to DNA but somewhat simpler in structure. This RNA would eventually become complex enough that it had all the functionalities of living creatures in it. That developed further — around three-and-a-half billion years ago — into the DNA and protein-based world that we have today, and you have this last common ancestor of all current life.

Having the right kind of chemicals around — how common is that on other planets? The right kind of chemistry is in fact debated. There are a couple of different scenarios. The scenario that I find most possible is the one pictured here, where the combination of a water-rich world and hydrogen cyanide turns out to be much better for originating of life and for sustaining it. It is abundant, and from this hydrogen cyanide-based chemistry can actually form all the building blocks of life as we know it today. Another way to ask this question is: How often do exoplanets have this water on them and have the right kind of chemistry?

This is an artist's impression of what it would be like to stand there on a planet, a perfectly temperate planet, around this very small star. As you can see, there's lots of water here because it's the right temperature to sustain liquid water. But just because you're at the right temperature doesn't mean that you actually have water around. The first question we can ask is how often planets form from material that is rich in water. If you look in the solar system, Earth is not one of the most water-rich bodies out there; some of the moons in the outer solar system have far more water for their size than Earth does. So at least where the earth was forming, in the disk where the earth was assembled, water must be very common. And if we look more generally in these discs where planets are currently forming, we can check how much water is there currently, where planet formation is happening, and the answer is that there's a lot. Here are two different ways that we use to look for water in these disks. One is to look for water vapor — that's what you see to your left. All those spikes that are not in red, green, or yellow are water vapor in one of these disks. Then to your right you see another spectra: this shows how you block or emit light at specific waving or colors due to having particular chemicals or species in these disks. And what you see are broad features in the spectra due to ice and material in this disk. We see there's lots of water and ice, both in solid and in gas form. We have a lot of water available where planets are forming.

We don't think that lack of water will be a problem for having life originate on other planets. How about the other part? We don't just need water, we also need hydrogen cyanide and other chemicals that are in this diagram. If we look with telescopes at these disks, if we look very carefully — do you see the kinds of molecules in these disks? To get this image, we have an amazing new telescope in Chile, the Atacama Large Millimeter and Submillimeter Array. What is so amazing about this telescope is that it was built to allow us to observe two things very carefully. One is the dust which tells us the overall structure, and the other is what molecules are in these disks. You already saw one example of a disk taken with ALMA. These are another twenty or so of them. I just want to pause and let us realize how amazing it is that we can now see planets forming in action. The lanes that are being carved out here are most likely baby planets that are carving out material as they are orbiting these young stars.

Now we can do more than just look at these disks and structures. We can also look for the light that's coming from specific molecules, and the kind of molecule that we were interested in — remember, it's hydrogen cyanide. And when we look for it, we do indeed find it. I mean, this is a cartoon, but we do see these hydrogen cyanide molecules in the disks. And it's there often, it's there in large abundance. If we put this together, what we have are lots of planets around young stars. Many of these planets seem to be at the right temperature to be habitable. They have the right temperature to sustain liquid water, to have the kind of life that we have here on Earth. We have also seen that water is abundant where planets are forming, and it's very likely that they are water-rich if they are at the right temperature. We've also seen that we often have the right organics, which means they are also likely to have the right building blocks for life. But what we don't know yet is if any of these planets are inhabited. That is something that hopefully we will find out over the next 20 to 30 years, but I don't think it's too early to start thinking about the possible consequences for our relationship with God.

There are two kinds of extraterrestrial life that we could find. One is bacterial or animal or vegetable life. On Earth it took a few hundred million years for that kind of life to first develop. A few hundred million years is a long time, but it is much, much, shorter than the four billion years for rational life to develop here on earth. It seems — but it's not obvious — that just because you develop life on a planet, you're going to develop the biologically machinery you need for rational life. Of course, we also believe that in addition to the biological machinery, you need God to especially create a rational soul for us, although whether He always does that is a pretty fair question to ponder. We might see life; we might see even intelligent life. What does this tell us about our place in the universe? That there are potentially living worlds; that we live in a universe potentially full of living worlds. It might seem that this makes us less important than we were 20 years ago. At least, that's an argument that you sometimes hear: that who are we to believe that we are especially loved and created by God, since we're tiny creatures on a tiny planet in the backwaters of this boring galaxy somewhere in the vast cosmos. First of all, I always say that Nazareth was also in the backwaters, so we should not be sad about being in the backwaters of our galaxy. But more than that, I think to claim that this is a new question is simply false. It's true that we today know that the universe is much, much, bigger than people did 3,000 years ago, but the universe has always been a big place. I mean, I like to go back to Psalm 8, where the psalmist, very rightly, I think, ponders: "When I see your heavens, the work of your fingers, the moon and stars that you set in place, what is man that you are mindful of him? And the son of man that you care for him?"

You don't need to know that the universe is billions of light years across to wonder why God would care about us. It might be that the discovery of exoplanets has made us seem less special than we were before. We believe that everything God creates shows, in some unique way, His glory. So there are aspects of His glory that are in these exoplanetary systems, and not just in ours. But I would say on the other hand that exoplanets have in some way made the universe a cozier place. I mean, when we're looking up at the skies, we no longer see cold stars — we see worlds surrounding their suns. What if they are inhabited? Well they might be. I would actually hope that they are. I think it would be wonderful to live in a universe teeming with life of all different kinds, of varieties. We still don't know if that is true. It might also be that we are the ark of the universe, carrying all the life that there is through space and time; and until we have discovered that there is alien life there, this is still a possibility that makes this world all the more precious.

I don't think anyone's really nervous about finding life on other places now. We expect bacteria. An interesting theological discussion arises from the possibility of extraterrestrial intelligent life. I think there are two questions that come up. One is how it affects our relationship with God; we are described as the crown of the creation in Genesis. That argument I don't find very troubling or convincing, I guess. We already know there's at least one other intelligent species in the universe and that has not in any way had a damaging effect on us. On the contrary, angels have been very helpful to us. We already know this universe is full of this alien species. That should be a comfort. But the other part has to do with the Incarnation, which I think is where trouble enters. Now, if there are other species out there, they may or may not have fallen, considering that there are only two intelligent species we know; although I guess every kind of angel is its own species. So it seems like it's not totally improbable that if you have another intelligent life that they would also have fallen, and therefore, you need to be saved. Could they have their own Incarnation? Some people believe yes. Theologians believe yes. I really encourage you to read a book by Marie I. George: *Christianity and Extraterrestrials? A Catholic Perspective*. It's a Thomistic analysis of aliens and it's fantastic. I would say no, because although God can of course do what He wants, it seems from scripture and from theology that this was a one-in-a-universe kind of event: God stepping down into His own creation to die. But then, if we have the inclination and other species don't, that seems incredibly unfair. They don't get a direct biological relationship with their Redeemer. They might not hear about Him for a million years — does that seem right? Then again, we, too, had to be grafted onto Israel, so it does not seem completely improbable that God would work out salvation for other species by grafting them onto humanity. A million years is a long time, but the people in my native Sweden had to wait 1,000 years before they found out about Christ. This seems a part of how God works; that He really likes working through a small group of people and saving the universe through them.

Finally, I just want to say that I would be extremely excited about an encounter with aliens. When we've encountered another intelligent species — angels — they've revealed things about God to us that we did not know before. I'm certain that if there are other rational species, then God has revealed Himself to them in some way, and getting to hear their stories about God would, I think, give us a whole new set of information and understanding of who God is as a creator. So with that positive ending, I'm going to hand it back to Massimo. [*audience applause*]

Robberto: I don't know what to add. I'm amazed and grateful, because this event gives us the possibility of meeting people like Professors Lunine and Öberg, and gives us the possibility of continuing this conversation among us. Thank you. [*audience applause*] It's always a cliché at such a moment to mention a guest's busy schedule, but really, he has an extraordinary schedule. He has come hurriedly from Barcelona to be a witness today and we are thrilled beyond words. Thank you. [*audience applause*]

An Irreducible Expectation

A conversation on the Encounter's theme. With **David Brooks**, *New York Times Editorialist;* **Fr. Javier Prades**, *President of the University of San Damaso, Madrid; and moderated by* **John Zucchi**, *History Professor, McGill University*

Introduction

"Cesare Pavese once wrote 'What a great thought it is that truly nothing is due to us. Has anyone ever promised us anything? Then why should we expect something?' Perhaps he did not realize that expectation is the very structure of our nature, it is the essence of our soul. It is not something calculated: it is given. For the promise is at the origin, from the very origin of our creation. He who has made man has also made him as 'promise.' Structurally, man awaits; structurally, he is a beggar; structurally, life is promise.

The religious sense is reason's capacity to express its own profound nature in the ultimate question; it is the 'locus' of consciousness that a human being has regarding existence. Such an inevitable question is in every individual, in the way he looks at everything. The Anglo-American philosopher Alfred N. Whitehead defines religion in this way: 'Religion is what the individual does with his own solitariness.' The definition, although interesting, does not fully express the value of the intuition that gave it birth. True, this ultimate question is indeed constitutive of the individual. And in that sense, the individual is totally alone. He himself is that question, and nothing else. For, if I look at a man, a woman, a friend, a passerby, without the echo of that question resounding within me, without that thirsting for destiny which constitutes him or her, then our relationship would not be human, much less loving at any level whatsoever. It would not, in fact, respect the dignity of the other, be suitable to the human dimension of the other. But that same question, in the very same instant that it defines my solitude, also

---

Saturday, February 16, 2019

establishes the root of my companionship, because this question means that I myself am constituted by something else mysterious."

~Luigi Giussani, *The Religious Sense*, McGill, 1997, pages 54; 56

❖   ❖   ❖   ❖   ❖

John Zucchi: Good afternoon and welcome to this session. My name is John Zucchi, I'm your moderator. On my right we have David Brooks, who became — [*audience applause*]. Well, he obviously needs no introduction. He is, as you know, a *New York Times* editorialist, a columnist. He also is a regular commentator on the *PBS Newshour* and NPR's *All Things Considered*. I have another 10 lines here I'm going to skip, and go straight to the little bio from his 2015 bestseller. He says: "I was born with a natural disposition towards shallowness. I now work as a pundit and columnist. I'm paid to be a narcissistic blowhard. [*audience laughter*] To volley my opinions, to appear more confident about them than I really am, to appear smarter than I really am, to appear better and more authoritative than I really am. I have to work harder than most people to avoid a life of smug superficiality." [*audience laughter*] Don't you want to hear from someone like that?

Fr. Javier Prades is on my left. He does not have an official bio, because he doesn't need a hook, he does academic, theological books. [*audience laughter*] Fr. Prades is a priest of the Diocese of Madrid, is the Director of the Department of Dogmatic Theology and Dean of the University of San Dámaso in Madrid. He is the author of several books and co-author — with Msgr. Luigi Giussani and Fr. Stefano Alberto — of *Generating Traces in the History of The World*, published by McGill-Queen's University Press. Welcome to our speakers. [*audience applause*]

In a recent piece in the *New York Times* entitled, "Life Without Longing," the poet and writer Melissa Broder talks about a life filled with yearning, with longing, and tries to understand what it is that we long for. She writes of romantic obsession and the need to be loved, and how this led her, in her life, to attempts at self-love. One little quote: "What would I have done if I had actually landed on some final, immutable me, whom I embraced with all my heart? For the sake of my own hunger for pursuit, I would have likely thrown her back in the water and kept looking. I would have been sad to give up the quest." She, like us, was looking, is looking for something. Like Pavese, what a great thought it is that truly nothing is due to us. Has anyone ever promised us anything? Then why should we expect something? We can't skip over this yearning, nor can we skip over this "something" that we all yearn for.

And so, David Brooks and Fr. Javier Prades: this will help us understand the "something" inside of us, and to appreciate its relevance for our times. David?

David Brooks: Thank you. It's a pleasure to be back at the Encounter. Two years ago, I was here for the first time, and Javier and I arrived at the same word when recalling it: "renewal." It's also a pleasure to be back on 18th Street. I grew up on 14th Street, four blocks away. When I was eight, I read a book called *Paddington Bear* and decided at that moment I wanted to become a writer. That was my annunciation moment and I've been writing ever since.

The first thing I want to say to you is, I'm not naturally a deep person. I'm naturally a rational, shallow person. When I was in high school there was a young woman named Bernice who I wanted to date, and she didn't want to date me, she wanted to date some other guy. I remember saying, "What is she thinking? I write way better than that guy!" [*audience laughter*] Writing was in my blood. When I was 18, the admissions officer said Columbia, Wesley, and then Brown. I decided I should go to the University of Chicago, about which there is a great saying: it's a Baptist school where atheist professors teach Jewish students St. Thomas Aquinas. [*audience laughter*]

That was my education, very cerebral. I had a double major in history and celibacy while I was at Chicago. I wasn't sure I should say that to a Catholic audience. [*audience laughter*] I went off on my cerebral way. I'm now a conservative columnist at the *New York Times*, which is a job I liken to being the chief rabbi in Mecca — not a lot of company there. I also work in TV, but even in TV I work in the bookish end of it. I'm on a show called the *NewsHour* on PBS, and we do a segment called "Shields and Brooks." We wanted to call it "Brooke Shields" because that would work better, but they didn't go for that. We cater to a cerebral audience, a somewhat older audience, so if a 93-year-old lady comes up to me in the airport, I know what she's going to say: "I don't watch your show but my mother loves it." [*audience laughter*] We're very big in the hospice community. So, books have been my life. I've tried to get a little more spiritual as I've gotten older, but it's just — I've become a little more feminine, I think. I'm the only American male to finish this book called *Eat, Pray, Love*, if you remember that book. By page 123 I was actually lactating, which is amazing. [*audience laughter*]

I wrote a book about emotion, and then I wrote about character, a book called *Road to Character*. I learned writing that book that writing up a kind character doesn't actually give you good character. And even reading a book about character doesn't give you good character. But, buying a book on character does give you good character. [*audience laughter*] So does buying the next book of the guy who wrote about character. So, let's say I've lived my life heads-up; yet I would have to say that the rational mind is only the third most important part of our consciousness. The first is our desiring heart, as Augustine taught us. I read about a guy who bought a house with a bamboo stand by the driveway, and he didn't like bamboo, so he chopped it down and axed the plants at the root system. He dug a three-foot hole, poured plant poison, three feet of gravel, six inches of cement, and two years later, a little shoot of bamboo sprouted up through the cement.

In my view, we all have that. We have the desires of our heart, which never go away. We are, as somebody said, existential sharks: we have to be on the move to live. What the heart yearns for more than anything else is fusion with another person. The kind of loving fusion that Louis de Bernières described in a book called *Captain Corelli's Mandolin*. In that book, he's got an old guy talking to his daughter about his relationship with his late wife, and the guy says, "Love itself is what is leftover when being in love has burned away, and this is both an art and a fortunate accident. Your mother and I had it, we had roots that grew towards each other underground, and when all the pretty blossoms had fallen from our branches we found that we were one tree and not two." So that's what the heart longs for.

The second part of the consciousness that forms our yearning is our soul. Now, unlike a lot of people in this room, I'm not in the business of persuading people that there's a God or not a God. But even before secular audiences I ask you to believe that you have a soul; that there's some piece of you that has no weight, size, color, or shape, but gives you infinite dignity. Rich and successful people don't have more of this than less successful people, old more than young. Slavery is wrong because it's an obliteration of another person's soul; rape is not just an attack on a bunch of physical molecules, it's an assault on someone's soul. And what this soul does is yearn, as the heart yearns for fusion with another, the soul yearns for fusion with the good. I've covered wars, I've covered crime, I've covered genocide. I've never met anybody who didn't want to be good. Even people who do very bad things have some rationalization to explain why it's actually good. What the soul yearns for is fusion towards some perfection, some moral perfection. The sort of perfection that Rabbi Wolfe Kelman tasted on the bridge at Selma with Dr. King. He said, "We felt connected, in song, to the transcendental, to the ineffable. We felt triumph and celebration. We felt that things change for the good and nothing is congealed forever. That was a warming, transcendental spiritual experience." Our heart and our soul are really the yearnings, the things that are pushing us forward, the things pointing to our ultimate ends, pointing not to a yearning and a longing, but a calling. Something at the ultimate end that's throwing us backwards. Our society does a very poor job of talking about the heart and soul. We have a lot of great scientists talking about cognition in the brain, our heuristics and our biases. We know almost nothing about our motivation; we don't tend to think about it, and as a result, our society has become something of a conspiracy against joy. We live in a society that's hyper-individualistic, that breaks off the connections between people and each other. And we see this in 45,000 suicides every year, 72,000 drug addiction deaths. People are just isolated and cut off from each other. I look at commencement speeches, which are American culture's chief sermon, and usually they hire someone with extreme career success to tell the students that career success doesn't matter. [*audience laughter*] Then they say, "Oh, don't be afraid to fail," and from this you learn that failure is really great if you happen to be J.K. Rowling. The rest? Don't fail. Failing is not good. But they give people the habits of our age. My students are wanting to know what to devote their lives to, what to commit to, what their lives are for. And we say, "Be free, be open." That does them no good. Freedom is what they're drowning in. They want to know what to devote themselves to. Then we say, "Your future is limitless." We give them this empty box of possibility and they say, "Yeah, I know I'm limitless, but I wanna know which life is right, and which life is wrong, and what my sources of authority should be." We give them the box of authenticity: "Look inside yourself, 'you do you,' find yourself, follow your passion." The "you" is the exact thing that's not been formed, and so they're drowning in freedom, drowning in possibility, looking for some sense of direction and guidance and wisdom, and we have nothing to say. Therefore some of them go off and lead an aesthetic life. They just treat life as a series of pleasures, one after the other, which never amounts to anything. Some of them become insecure overachievers. They decide they can solve the problem at their moral foundation if they build one success on top of the other. My students come back years after graduation and call me, and very often their voices have been crushed because they've had a setback. Nietzsche says, "He who has a 'why' to live for can endure any 'how.'" If you know your ultimate end, you can endure the setbacks, but if you haven't, you get crushed. I have a friend that lives in town here named Casey Gerald, who was at a job interview once, and he turned around and asked the interviewer a question. "What would you do if you weren't afraid?" And she started crying. Because if she wasn't afraid, she wouldn't be doing HR at that company.

What they suffer from is what the Catholic Church used to call acedia — the loss of desire. Your life is over here, but your heart is over there. I say this about the younger generation, but I'm no different than anybody else. I grew up with the writer's personality. To be a good writer, it really helps to be aloof and a little cut off from other people. I tell young journalists, if you're at a football game, and everyone else is doing the wave and you just sit there, then you have the right aloof personality type to become a journalist. [*audience laughter*] A friend of mine named Christian Wiman says the reason a lot of us write is because we can't really relate to people socially. We need some way to connect, so we do it through our pen. Wiman writes, "A certain emotional reserve in one's life becomes a source of great power in one's work." So, we're sort of solitary to start with, and then we've got a profession that keeps us alone all day. John Cheever was a writer who would get up — he had a Park Avenue apartment — put on a suit, and rode down to the basement where his typewriter was. He took off his suit and wrote in his boxers. At noon, he put back on the suit, rode up the elevator and had lunch alone. That's the writer's life. And then if you succeed, they send you on a book tour. I was on book tour from my last book 99 days in a row, 6:00 a.m. flights every morning. I counted 142 meals alone at airports. If you remember, Britney Spears shaved off her head, totally went crazy. I was like, Yeah, I get that. I'm like that. [*audience laughter*] A lot of what the meritocracy does is shave us to be aerodynamic, to glide upward. Not to attach, but to rise. And in my case, I came to desire the wrong things. I came to desire reputation: How am I doing? How well known am I? Is my column being read? More poisonously, I came to idolize time over people. I came to want to be so productive, and my relationships slipped away. And the wages of sin are sin, and you wind up in the depths. In 2013, I was in the depths. My marriage had ended, my kids had left for college, my friendships were mostly in conservative circles and conservatism has changed. I lived alone in an apartment, and if you opened up the kitchen drawers in my apartment, where you should've found silverware you found Post-It notes. Where you should have found plates, you found envelopes. That was a life consumed by work and nothing else. You know what I learned in that? I had total freedom. I was alone. I had money, I had some reputation. I was free; we're in a society that tells you to want freedom. And I learned in those years that freedom sucks. Political freedom is great; personal freedom sucks. Don't be unattached. The unattached person is the unremembered person.

But it gave me renewed insight into moral renewal, which comes in three phases, and I'll just end with these three phases. One, it breaks you open. People in times of suffering are either broken or they're broken open. If they're broken, they shrivel. If they're broken open, they grow. Paul Tillich, the 1950s theologian, said that what suffering does is remind you you're not the person you thought you were. It carves through the floor in the basement of your soul; it carves through that floor and reveals a cavity below, and when you see those unexpected depths in yourself, you realize that only spiritual food will fill those cavities. It shatters the illusion of self-sufficiency. It sends you into exile from the regular flow of your normal life and sends you out into the wilderness. In moments of suffering, there's this weird mixture, where some of the time you've really got to be with people, but some of the time you've really got to be alone. In the Jewish tradition, there is a story of Moses when he was in the wilderness. He had a little lamb in his flock, and the lamb took off. Lambs are not normally that fast, but this lamb took off like a gazelle, and Moses ran after and chased it deeper, deeper, deeper into the wilderness. The rabbis teach us the lamb was Moses himself — he had to go deeper into the wilderness to find himself. And what's out there in the wilderness? The first thing that's out there is: there's nobody to applaud your performance, and that's why solitude is necessary. The second thing that's out there is the sort of suffering that cracks through the ego shell. And the third thing that's out there is the thing that takes you deepest, back to yourself, to the heart and soul. Annie Dillard wrote, "In the deeps are the violence and terror of which psychology has warned us. But if you ride these monsters deeper down, if you drop with them farther over the world's rim, you find what our sciences cannot name: the substrate, the ocean, or matrix, which buoys all the rest, which gives goodness its power for good, and evil its power for evil, the unified field, our complex, inexplicable caring for each other." And this is Augustine: you go down into yourself, and you find down in yourself a highway right out of self. Because you find your heart and soul, which long to attach to one another. But you have to be broken open.

And then the second thing you find is, after you're broken open, you still need somebody to help you out. In my view, nobody can lead themselves out of the wilderness. They need somebody else to reach in and grab them out. I was grabbed out by three things. One was a community called AOK, a group of young people in Washington, D.C., with whom I had dinner every Thursday night and still do. They're young kids, often from very broken homes. I went there the first time five years ago. I reached out my hand to introduce myself to one of these kids. He said, "We don't really shake hands, we hug here." I'm not the most huggy guy on the face of the earth, but I hug them, and they have a complete intolerance of social distance. They turn to you, hungering for love like flowers toward the sun, and they pulled me out.

My love for my wife pulled me out. What love for a man or a woman does is shave off the topsoil, the crusty stuff on top, and exposes the soft stuff below. It reminds you that your riches are outside yourself. The other thing about love is it wants to be on the move. A love for a person wants to lead upward to a higher love. And so the third thing that pulls you out is God. Some people find God in suffering, in the depths, and they feel humble and they need His help, and I get that. I've always liked the best of God's offers. I've always liked the vision of goodness and transcendence and joy. I'm somehow more inspired by that. There was a woman who lived down here — I hope you all know her and have read her — named Dorothy Day. Toward the end of her life she was asked, "Are you going to write a memoir?" And she said, "Well, I tried to write one once." She was asked by a guy named Robert Coles, and she said, "I sat there and I wrote 'A Life to Remember' on the top of the page, and I sat there and tried to think of what to write, and I thought of the Lord, and His visit to us all those centuries ago. I was just grateful to have had Him on my mind all that time." And she realized she didn't need to write anything. That serenity pulls you forward.

The second thing that you sometimes see is a moral beauty, a transcendence, a spiritual divine. I'm sure a lot of you know Henri Nouwen's work. My favorite Nouwen story: he was at L'Arche already, but when he would go off to speak, he would bring a member of this community, a mentally disabled man, with him. He was going to Washington to give a speech and he brought a man named Bill. When Nouwen came up on stage, Bill came up on stage. Nouwen spoke and Bill sat behind him, and when Bill heard something he'd heard before from Nouwen, he would tell the audience, "I've heard that before," and then at the end of Nouwen's speech, Bill said, "I would like to give a speech, too." Nouwen was a little nervous; Bill was mentally disabled, and he didn't know what Bill would say. He might ramble on embarrassingly. So, Bill said, "Last time Henri went to Boston, he took John Smeltzer with him. This time he wanted me to come with him to Washington. I'm very glad to be here with you. Thank you very much" — and he sat down. And the audience gave him a standing ovation. After it was all over, Bill worked the room. [*audience laughter*] Met everybody he could, shook hands, signed autographs. The next day at breakfast, Nouwen and Bill were leaving for the airport, but Bill wanted to say goodbye to everybody, so he worked the room, the breakfast room at the hotel. As they were flying home, Bill asked Nouwen if he liked the trip. Nouwen said, "Oh yes, it was a wonderful trip. I'm so glad you came with me." Bill said, "And we did it together, didn't we?" Nouwen thought of Jesus's words: "Where two or three meet in my name, I am among them." That's the kind of moral sublime that touches something deep in ourselves and calls us to our end. Thank you.

Fr. Javier Prades: I am truly grateful to the organizers of the NYE for the possibility to share this roundtable today with David Brooks and with all of you. It is a great honor to share the table with a figure of such contemporary relevance, and it is a joy to come back and see so many dear faces, with the sense that some new friendship may also emerge. I will give an initial presentation with five main points, in order to nurture a common dialogue.

A landscape of uncertainty

In his posthumous 2014 book, *The Metamorphosis of the World,* the late German sociologist Ulrich Beck opens with a statement that affects us all: "The world has gone berserk….it is disjointed and has gone mad." He acknowledges that his sociological formation does not provide a simple answer to the question, "What is the meaning of the global events that unfold before our eyes on television screens?" The world is no longer comprehensible to him. The usual sociological categories for describing sociological phenomena — evolution, revolution, and transformation — seem insufficient to explain the world that we have before us today. Beck thus incorporates into sociological language the category of "metamorphosis." With it, he means to express not that the world is dying, but that, rather, it "is experiencing a radical transformation, a metamorphosis of the horizon of references and action coordinates…" In virtue of which "the old certainties of modern society are disappearing, while something totally new is emerging." His book is an explicit effort at finding a way to respond to this confusion and the sense of discomfort that accompanies it. This is the point of view that interests us: What is the collective diagnosis of our global situation? Believers, agnostics, and atheists alike are part of these secular and post-secular pluralistic societies of the West.

The Polish philosopher and sociologist Zygmunt Baumann offered a description similar to Beck's, when he warned that — at least in the countries considered "developed"— we have entered into a scenario characterized by uncertainty, by insecurity. After the apparent solidity of modernity, we have entered into a liquid and insubstantial period of time, where numerous social forms appear incapable of offering realms of certainty or reference points for human action. The root of this uncertainty is found in "our way of living," distinguishable "for the weakening of interpersonal ties, the collapse of communities, the substitution of competition without limits for solidarity, the tendency to trust the problems of greatest impact to the hands of private individuals." Bauman directs his attention to this emptying of the human, personal, and social fabric, which sustained Europe for centuries and which results in an uncertainty that affects all aspects of life.

We find ourselves in "post-secular" society, with an outlook constituted by personal and social insecurity, caused fundamentally by the disappearance of many of the certainties on which people built their lives. The evidence for human values is discussed and debated, as we see in the many debates over what is reason, or what is freedom, or what value representative democracy has versus the liberal social state of law, or community life versus that of every individual. As Peter Berger warned, we are not facing a minor problem; we are facing a difficulty with very serious social consequences, since as we lose these certainties, we excavate what he referred to as "the moral consensus without which no society can endure."

Here is where I will locate my reflections, in order to contribute to understanding and moving beyond this difficulty we all share, starting precisely from the originality of Christianity. In dialoguing with the positions I have laid out, I want us to take note of the voices pointing us to what is at stake: the disappearance of shared certainties, on which the future of humanity — inasmuch as it is truly human — rests.

"Spaces of Action"

The first thing I want to affirm is that, in order to move beyond the current state of things, mere reflection is not enough. While a conceptual elaboration is indispensable, and it influences our action, what is required is something like what Beck refers to as "cosmopolitan spaces of action," understood as "existential parameters of social activity." Without claiming to transpose this sociological concept, it suggests that the changes in the many worldviews do not come primarily from the elaboration of an alternative theory, but rather from what Beck calls "creative action" in the world connected in cosmopolitan fashion, where such action does not accept "the current frontiers of thought and action." There is, therefore, a space of opportunity for those who enter into the cosmopolitan world starting from their creative action, starting from their own experience and what — in the language of believers — we could call their lived witness.

The aim of this hyperconnected world, exposed to the temptations of extremism, becomes an opportunity to offer an understanding of what is human that avoids an elitist and exclusive worldview. That "space of action" can orient us in the direction of what the Spanish sociologist Manuel Castells refers to as "united forms of life…[which are]…rooted in our souls," and which counterbalance the "collapse of communities" and the tendency — which we saw Bauman warn against — to delegate the solution of our most serious problems to private individuals. In this situation, in fact, the metamorphosis is something not merely to suffer through, but even to encourage with great hope.

From these "spaces of action" oriented towards the human horizon, it makes sense to think again about the role of religion in the post-secular world. The role of religion need not be confined, for example, to debates on bioethical questions, as Habermas suggests; rather, it can provide places for personal and social construction, humanizing spaces that encompass all aspects of life. If time allows, I will return to this angle later on.

The weakening of the self and of the community
Bauman, Castells, and Habermas have all noted the weakening of human communities as spaces capable of developing free people. While Beck seems, instead, to emphasize the primacy of individual experience, and sees community dimension as derived from that experience, the importance of the "spaces of action" that he advocates clearly demonstrate a community dimension.

We should really take the time for a careful study of the relationship between the individual and the communal dimension in human experience. Taking it as a given for now, we will give priority to consideration of this "weakening" of the human dimension, considering particularly the aspect of each person, of each "self," while also offering social lines of action of a clearly communal nature.

I share the diagnosis that there has been a weakening of communal ties in the Western world. In my view, it is a reflection, among other factors, of the weakening of what Luigi Giussani calls "elementary experience." With this term, he refers to the very core of needs and evidence at the heart of a person's relation to reality: truth, justice, freedom, goodness — and which are not satisfied by possessing any object within our reach, but rather, always beckon to something "beyond." In using the concept of experience, Giussani suggests that it is not so much a problem of establishing a theory of man, but of observing his concrete situation in history, which is always open to a greater fulfillment. A reflection on the human comes while man is living, once he is placed in action on the world stage — on what the great Spanish playwright Calderón called the "gran teatro del mundo." To put it in another way, it is necessary to be living, in the midst of the drama of life, with all its concrete relationships and circumstances, in order to be surprised by what actually fulfills the human vision of what we sense as an original promise of happiness. It is worthwhile to really understand the nature of this experience, since if we do not keep all of its elements in mind, an insistence on the "personal" moment will only lead to what are individualistic, and ultimately narcissistic, positions, incapable of social construction. Elementary experience is a person's own experience, but it is not private; rather, it opens onto all dimensions of reality.

The Spanish philosopher Maria Zambrano already warned us years ago of the risk of impoverishing our elementary experience. I quote her directly: "What is in crisis is this mysterious nexus that unites our being with reality, something so deep and essential that is our inner sustenance." We call it "a weakening of the self," but this crisis affects our sense of the world, of others and of our very being, keeping us on the rigid or ideological surface of things, thereby shown to be living in uncertainty. Zambrano's is a timely warning that this means losing our "inner sustenance," because reality nourishes us when it puts us in contact with this enigmatic "something more," which we could call Mystery.

Despite the frequency with which cultural or psychological causes are mentioned as the root of this weakening, its true root is epistemological and anthropological. It comes from the difficulty in recognizing and welcoming reality in the way in which it immediately appears, without burdening it with the measure of what someone thinks they already know beforehand; reality that awakens admiration precisely because it is given, and, at the same time, corresponds to the rational structure of every person. An adequate understanding of human elementary experience, capable of perceiving the mysterious nature of reality, and, in particular, this point of reality that is each one of us, can tackle the questions of all sorts that contact with the real inevitably produces in every human person's reason. In light of this thesis, it would be useful to review in detailed fashion what Charles Taylor calls "exclusive humanism," and show, in line with his analysis, that exclusive humanism is truly not a genuine understanding of what is human. A step in this same direction would be to listen to those who, from different perspectives, have underscored the legitimacy of questions about the ultimate meaning of life, who have been a continual source of the search for truth, especially in the history of philosophy. Figures as different as George Steiner, Eric Voegelin, or Ludwig Wittgenstein have claimed, in different ways, the legitimacy of those questions. Perhaps I should include David Foster Wallace in this list as well. I should add some exceptional women to that list, too, like the previously cited Maria Zambrano, as well as Hannah Arendt, Edith Stein, Etty Hillesum, and Flannery O'Connor, who have offered different paths to an understanding of visible reality that is not enough on its own, a reality that refers back to a Mystery without which we could not even understand convincingly what we see.

By means of a "recognition in action"

How can we recognize human characteristics, that is to say, the needs and evidence specific to "elementary experience" on a personal and social level so as to overcome the aforementioned weakening of the self? We should return to the classical task of reflecting on the observations about human nature. But is it possible to do so at this point in time, when the common evidence about what it means to be human, that we once shared, seems to have dissolved in a sea of pluralistic positions, when they aren't contradicting each other? What is the appropriate method?

In light of the above, it seems clear that this method can no longer consist in the application of a system of ideas and predetermined values that are "abstract," to put it one way. Indeed, in order to achieve effective social transmission of the principles, values, and ideals that establish a culture, including the religious ones, it is not sufficient to move within the theoretical level, comparing intellectual constructions, in order to determine which contains the most truth. Without going into all the necessary speculative implications, it seems unquestionable that the assimilation of a value relevant to society such as truth, justice, happiness, or also friendship, or maternity, or freedom — universals in their own right, inasmuch as they are part of the "elementary experience" of every man — will not occur efficiently if that assimilation doesn't begin in the concrete experience of having friends, or having a mother, or meeting someone who is free. It is not enough, for example, for a child to be taught in school that mothers ought to love their children; the child needs to experience being loved. It is only in this way that the child could recognize and know what it means to be loved by a mother; if not, he cannot understand it properly.

The most appropriate method for effectively transmitting values involves at least two dimensions.

In first place, a pedagogy that allows the "recognition in act" of common values and shared human characteristics is indispensable. When I say "recognition," I'm not just talking about an arbitrary consensus, as the common usage of this category suggests. When I say "in act," I mean that true education does not limit itself to simply repeating exact ideas about human nature but rather allows for the identification of the intellectual content of each truth from lived experience of the common human value in question. The anthropological motive that underlies this educational conception — as I already said — is that the human being, when he questions himself, always does so from the here and now of his own existence, both in a personal way and in community.

Having said that, secondly, we must realize that human ideals and values do not appear to the discerning subject, no matter how prepared and open he is, "in a pure state," so to speak, but rather they are assimilated concretely and according to the traits of a concrete human tradition, cultural or religious. For this reason, it is indispensable that the recognition in act of these universal values occur from within what is often called the "narration" of one's lived tradition. It is in this sense that I wanted to speak at the beginning about the necessary principle of "spaces of action," in which universal values are present in a concrete form. In this way, the existence of other potential traditions of values within the same plural society can be respected, and a space can emerge for legitimate debate about their greater or lesser suitability to express the fullness of human life. This approach avoids the imposition of one tradition over another and avoids falling into the relativism of mere cultural juxtaposition. What is promoted here is the virtuous exchange appropriate to a truly plural society in which democracy, as a universal value, is lived out with the backing of the "dominant tradition" that confers the greatest social legitimacy to legal and political proceedings. Both aspects of this method are necessary. On the one hand, the exercise of a personal recognition of the "correspondence" — *adaequatio* — between the social practice of a value and the elemental structure of the human experience; on the other hand, the narration of the communal, social, cultural, and religious context that makes it effectively possible. One must be able to understand, in a personal way, through the exercise of one's own reason, that friendship or maternity or freedom are undeniable dimensions of a full human experience, and therefore universal values. And this effective recognition is only possible where there is a particular context that narrates the effective experiences of free men, of true friends, of mothers that love their children.

With regard to the Christian tradition, this double criterion has always, in my opinion, formed part of the Church's task of transmitting the faith and customs, as far as it implies the reality of a particular historical and cultural context in which "a new humanity" with a universal scope takes shape. This new humanity, which represents a fullness according to the measure of Christ, takes shape thanks to an overabundance, beyond mere natural experience, from the gratuitous initiative of God.

The cognitive value of a personal encounter with the Truth
I have maintained that reflecting is not enough for discovering or rediscovering the original characteristics of elementary human experience. We need a "space of action" that allows for a new intelligence in regards to itself and the world, thanks to a web of relationships. In order to arrive at

the fullness that our human experience desires, it is not possible to deduce things, starting from principles — even if they are the right principles. Rather, it is necessary to discover in action if there is something that, in fact, fulfills and even exceeds that highest longing, a longing reflected in our elementary needs and evidence.

Put in simple terms, something has to happen in your personal life. We need a humanly significant "encounter," precisely because the self matures in its capacity of knowing both reality and itself through a relationship with others, who put the self in movement. The self is fulfilled in a "you" that the self recognizes as its own completeness. This is confirmed in many examples of daily life, where, thanks only to the value of an encounter with another, a person acquires or regains his self-confidence, the intellectual and emotional energy necessary to deal again with human life. The lived experiences of maternal love, of a friendship, of a relationship with a great teacher, give witness to this. This condition, specific to the human sphere, is what the Christian proposal must fulfill if it wants serve the social wellbeing of the West.

In this sense, in front of the great existential questions to which the authors I referred to at the beginning spoke about, the Christian proposal is to proclaim the initiative of the Mystery — God — that can be humanly received in a way similar to the way in which we receive other concrete forms of knowledge: by means of a personal recognition starting from an intersubjective, social context. Indeed, in line with the Christian proclamation, every human being has access to the unrepeatable content of his being, in virtue of a specific event that happens in history. All people have access to the fulfillment of the promise intuited through their elementary needs and evidence, thanks to the relationship with the Mystery, God, through the historical singularity of Jesus Christ and for the gift of His Spirit, which makes its presence known in history by means of the ecclesial community.

In truth, everything I have said today has been born from a network of relationships, of friendships that brought me here from Madrid, thanks to which I have been able to know and to love Christ, to the point of desiring that His good presence be with me always, and wanting that something like this should happen to everyone here, to all the men and women who live in the world. We can now continue the conversation with some questions. Thank you!

Zucchi: Thank you to David Brooks and Fr. Javier Prades. I was struck by how, from two very different talks, how we had some important issues that emerged from it. The one that struck me, that we cannot have certainty without undergoing an experience. We need to undergo an experience and we need to also see and experience in action. David, when you spoke about the crisis among young people nowadays, it was a prism into our current society and the divisions, polarization aside, the confusion, the ambiguities there. You responded by speaking very personally about yourself and your discovering your desires, going to the depths of yourself in experience. I want to know in our current cultural moment, do you have an example you can think of, that made it clear to you, of having something to start from, or something in which we can perceive a promise in our society here in North America or in Europe, or anywhere in the world?

Brooks: Well, in covering politics, I'm actually wildly and probably unrealistically optimistic about where we're going, in part because the master trend here, I think, in Western society, is the rise of a culture of individualism. A culture that says life is an individual journey; the essential social unit is the individual chooser, and that the question in life is, "What can I do to make myself happy?" I think we're seeing the fruits of that. We're seeing the weakening of social connections, and I think, as Fr. Prades said, the emphasis on the self leads to a weakening of the self, and a dissolution of the self, and a diminution of self-experience. When you emphasize the individual chooser, you lose touch with the heart and soul. You lose touch with the deepest part of yourself, and I think we're at the end of that. What I see all around me and, frankly, in this room, is a movement of people gathering and saying that the individual is not the essential unit of society, but rather the *relationship* is the essential unit of society. Both the relationship with each other and with some Almighty. What I think this room represents is, frankly, Catholic social thought in physical form, like the Catholic social teaching of personalism, like Jacques Maritain and Dorothy Day, who emphasized that the person is a move outward toward Other. I see that here, but in my daily life I see it in secular form in the group of community builders who I now spend my life traveling with. I do work at the Aspen Institute, on something called Weave: The Social Fabric Project. We go around in community, looking for communities all around the country, that in this context are like little mini-Cometas; that is to say, mini-second families where people have given themselves up to community, and you can find them everywhere. There's a kid in D.C. who lost his father when he was nine; his father was murdered by his mistress, and the son now works at a football camp, making sure other young men have adult figures. A woman I interviewed in Ohio had the worst thing that can happen to her: her husband killed their kids and then himself. She has devoted her life to service, to teaching pharmacy, to school. These people are everywhere. They're a movement that doesn't yet know it's a movement, but they're the living response to an error of excessive individualism. And my basic view is that people figure stuff out; and that a search for community led me to people I'd never heard of, like Jacques Maritain or Augustine. The yearning of the heart and the soul essentially pulls you back towards a society that's fit for a human being and fit for human dignity. I just think that is the way that this movement is part of a movement of social and spiritual recovery.

Zucchi: Thank you. Fr. Prades, I want to ask you a personal question. Just looking back at your life, can you pinpoint a juncture, a moment, in which this irreducible expectation became something very clear, very urgent for you?

Prades: Well, yesterday when I was landing at JFK, I remembered that the first time I came to America I was 14. I was so astonished landing in New York the first time. I came from a Spain still ruled by Franco, and for me it was a kind of a dream, sightseeing in Manhattan with open eyes. It seemed that, for the first time in my life, I felt there was something great around, something worthwhile to fight for and to aspire to. It became a kind of expectation, which remained in the following years. In the beginning, I think I identified this expectation, this longing for something great, as the image of myself being successful, or being rich, or being both. [*audience laughter*] For us — and I speak for myself, my generation — it was encouraged by our parents, who were all Catholics, that we should aim high, and work for a great fulfillment of life. There is a moment when you have to choose, and this is perhaps the first moment I noticed that there was something beyond. New York, success — these were not enough. And for years, there was a kind of obscure certainty. I could not put it in words. It's only after 55 years that I can give words to that experience. I was 14 when I came here for the first time; d until 16 or 17 there was a kind of fight in myself. If someone had asked me, "How do you feel?" I would have said, "Very well," but deep in my heart I was trying to identify an answer to the question deep in my heart. And this is why I say I had an encounter with something bigger than New York City. And you cannot earn money enough, not even here, to pay for it. [*audience applause*]

Zucchi: It remains for me to thank our two speakers for not having simply given us a talk, but for having invited us into the kitchen of their lives, invited us to look at their experience, what they are living, and we can leave here more certain and happier as well. Thank you, David Brooks, and thank you, Fr. Javier Prades. [*audience applause*]

Poetry: The Language of Human Longing

A presentation by **Paul Mariani**, *Poet, and introduced by Rita Simmonds, Poet*

Introduction

"It is this immortal instinct for beauty that thrusts us to regard the world and all its splendors as a reverberation, a resonance of heaven. The unquenchable thirst for all that is beyond, and which unveils life, is the most vivid proof of our immortality. It is at once by way of poetry and through poetry, as with music, that the soul glimpses splendors from beyond the tomb; and when an exquisite poem brings one's eyes to the point of tears, those tears are not evidence of an excess of joy, they are witness far more to an exacerbated melancholy, a disposition of the nerves, a nature exiled among imperfect things, which would like to possess, without delay, a paradise revealed on this very same earth."

~C. Baudelaiare, *Art Romantique:* "Notes nouvelles sur Edgar Poe III," IV

❖ ❖ ❖ ❖ ❖

Rita Simmonds: Good evening, and welcome everyone. You should find on your chairs a card about a publication called *Presence*, a journal of Catholic poetry. I want to thank Mary Ann Miller and all the people at *Presence* for helping to sponsor this event. Tonight's distinguished guest, Paul Mariani, is going to speak about poetry and read a few poems. I'm going to give you a very brief biography of Mr. Mariani. He is a poet, an author of many books, and Professor Emeritus of English at Boston College. He has too many achievements to name, but I would like to name just one: this September, he will be awarded the Lifetime Achievement Award from the Catholic Imagination Conference at Loyola University in Chicago. [*audience applause*] We are really extremely blessed and privileged to have him with us this evening. Paul Mariani. [*audience applause*]

Paul Mariani: Thank you very much. Let me begin this evening by quoting from the Austrian Catholic philosopher, Josef Seifert, who heads up the John Paul II Academy for Human Life and the Family. "Authentic hope," he reminds us, "begins with our power to realize what is good. Hope, therefore, must be reasonable to be desirable, and must be directed to other persons on whom the realization of our good aspirations depends. Therefore, the better and more perfect the person in whom we put our hope and the mightier he or she is, the more rational is our hope. Hope can only meaningfully be directed to a person, and to a completely trustworthy person who can grant us what we hope for. Hope, to make sense, presupposes a good and loving God. Placing all our hope in human ingenuity, good will, and power is illusory…"

There are two lights, St. Bonaventure tells us. If you once have seen the world in the light of the sun, you'll also see much more of it in the far weaker light of the moon and the stars at night. Just so. Once reality has been illumined by divine revelation, you will also see much more of it by human reason. As Saint John Paul put it: if we love, we cannot hope for the good of our beloved less than for our own. Hope is wholly permeated by love that extends to the other's happiness as well.

Fr. Michael Casey, a Cistercian monk of the Tarrawarra Abbey in Australia, has this to say about our encounter with the divine. Jesus, he reminds us, did promise us something to start from. That the Father, our Father, was willing to risk everything to bring us home and has already done so many times. It is in God's tender care for every one of us, for every family and community, that we invest our hope for the future. And so we take comfort. Our distinctive, unique experience, God's in-stressing — to use Hopkins' word — itself upon us, which seemed to come first in the ladder of hope. The sacred word would be the second step of revelation, offered as an explanation that keeps on giving what God has given us. And there is poetry which can give us something to start from.

Here are just a few of many examples. First, from other poets, and then some words in which I try to express my own sense of hope as a poet for whom the Catholic faith, even when I myself fall short, has always been paramount. The first poem I'd like to read is by my neighbor, Emily Dickinson, up there in Amherst. [*audience laughter*] It's called "Hope."

Hope is the thing with feathers —
That perches in the soul —
And sings the tune without the words —
And never stops — at all —

And sweetest — in the Gale — is heard —
And sore must be the storm —
That could abash the little Bird
That kept so many warm —

I've heard it in the chillest land —
And on the strangest Sea —
Yet, never, in Extremity,
It asked a crumb — of Me.

The second one is from Mary Oliver, who just passed very recently. It's called "Wild Geese."

You do not have to be good.
You do not have to walk on your knees
for a hundred miles through the desert repenting.
You only have to let the soft animal of your body
love what it loves.
Tell me about despair, yours, and I will tell you mine.
Meanwhile the world goes on.
Meanwhile the sun and the clear pebbles of the rain
are moving across the landscapes,
over the prairies and the deep trees,
the mountains and the rivers.
Meanwhile the wild geese, high in the clean blue air,

are heading home again.
Whoever you are, no matter how lonely,
the world offers itself to your imagination,
calls to you like the wild geese, harsh and exciting —
over and over announcing your place
in the family of things.

The third example is by Marie Howe, it's called "The Star Market."

The people Jesus loved were shopping at the Star Market yesterday.
An old lead-colored man standing next to me at the checkout
breathed so heavily I had to step back a few steps.
Even after his bags were packed he still stood, breathing hard and
hawking into his hand. The feeble, the lame, I could hardly look at them:
shuffling through the aisles, they smelled of decay, as if the Star Market
had declared a day off for the able-bodied, and I had wandered in
with the rest of them — sour milk, bad meat —
looking for cereal and spring water.
Jesus must have been a saint, I said to myself, looking for my lost car
in the parking lot later, stumbling among the people who would have
been lowered into rooms by ropes, who would have crept
out of caves or crawled from the corners of public baths on their hands
and knees begging for mercy.
If I touch only the hem of his garment, one woman thought,
could I bear the look on his face when he wheels around?
And then a poem by Amiri Baraka, Preface to a Twenty Volume Suicide Note,
and it's for Kellie Jones — that's his daughter — who was born 16 May 1959.
He's an angry man, but so gentle in this poem.
Preface to a Twenty Volume Suicide Note
Lately, I've become accustomed to the way
The ground opens up and envelopes me
Each time I go out to walk the dog.
Or the broad edged silly music the wind
Makes when I run for a bus...
Things have come to that.
And now, each night I count the stars,
And each night I get the same number.

And when they will not come to be counted,
I count the holes they leave.

Nobody sings anymore.
And then last night, I tiptoed up
To my daughter's room and heard her
Talking to someone, and when I opened
The door, there was no one there…
Only she on her knees, peeking into
Her own clasped hands.

And the final poem by someone else is by my favorite, Gerard Manley Hopkins. It's called "Carrion Comfort." We don't know the exact date; he just left it on a piece of paper and it was found after his death. It's 1885, Hopkins' father is about 40, 41 years old, and he's stationed in Dublin at a time of a great deal of unrest because of the Irish conditions. You're going to hear Jacob wrestling with the angel in this poem, and at the very end you'll hear the *Eli, Eli, lema sabachthani* — "My God, my God, why have you forsaken me?"

Not, I'll not, carrion comfort, Despair, not feast on thee;
Not untwist — slack they may be — these last strands of man
In me ór, most weary, cry I can no more. I can;
Can something, hope, wish day come, not choose not to be.
But ah, but O thou terrible, why wouldst thou rude on me
Thy wring-world right foot rock? lay a lionlimb against me? scan
With darksome devouring eyes my bruisèd bones? and fan,
O in turns of tempest, me heaped there; me frantic to avoid thee and flee?

Why? That my chaff might fly; my grain lie, sheer and clear.
Nay in all that toil, that coil, since (seems) I kissed the rod,
Hand rather, my heart lo! lapped strength, stole joy, would laugh, chéer.
Cheer whom though? the hero whose heaven-handling flung me, fóot tród
Me? or me that fought him? O which one? is it each one? That night, that year
Of now done darkness I wretch lay wrestling with (my God!) my God.

[audience applause]

105

That's a hard act to follow. Now I'll read some of my poems. The first one is called "Then Sings My Soul." It was written for a dear old friend of mine, Leonardo. It was written years ago when I was at a men's retreat in Cursillo, and he was dying at that point. The miracle is, his wife kept praying for him and he's still alive — he's 90 now. That was 40 years ago. I just saw him at the last men's retreat; they wheeled him in just so we could be together for one hour before he had to return. This is a poem I wrote for him. and it comes from that song, *Then Sings My Soul*.

Who can tell a man's real pain
— or a woman's either — when they learn
the news at last that they must die? Sure
we all know none of us is going anywhere

except in some pineslab box or its fine
expensive equal. But don't we put it off
another day, and then another and another,
as I suppose we must to cope? And so

with Lenny, Leonardo Rodriquez, a man
in the old world mold, a Spaniard
of great dignity and fine humility,
telling us on this last retreat for men

that he had finally given up praying
because he didn't want to hear
what God might want to tell him now:
that he wanted Lenny soon in spite

of the hard facts that he had his kids,
his still beautiful wife, and an aged
mother to support. I can tell you now
it hit us hard him telling us because
for me as for the others he'd been
the model, had been a leader, raised
in the old faith of San Juan de la Cruz
and Santa Teresa de Avila, this toreador

waving the red flag at death itself,
horns lowered and hurling down on him.
This story has no ending because there is
still life and life means hope. But

on the third day, in the last Mass, we were
all sitting in one big circle like something
out of Dante — fifty laymen, a priest, a nun —
with Guido DiPietro playing his guitar

and singing an old hymn in that tenor voice
of his, all of us joining in at the refrain,
Then sings my soul, my Savior God to thee,
How great thou art, how great thou art ,

and there I was on Lenny's left, listening
to him sing, his voice cracked with resignation,
how great thou art, until angry glad tears
began rolling down my face, surprising me. . . .

Lord, listen to the sound of my voice.
Grant Lenny health and long life. Or,
if not that, whatever strength and peace
he needs. His family likewise, and

his friends. Grant me too the courage
to face death when it shall notice me,
when I shall still not understand why
there is so much sorrow in the world.

Teach me to stare down those lowered horns
on the deadend street that shall have no alleys
and no open doors. And grant me the courage
then to still sing to thee, how great thou art.

[audience applause]

Thank you. The next poem is one I wrote this past September for my mother, for the memory of my mother, Harriet Mariani, who lived from March 6, 1923, to September 16, 1988.

Mid-September, dear woman
and the monarch lights
once more upon the purple,
powdery butterfly bush
in the now decaying garden
as it has for the past thirty Septembers.

And once again, like the softest breeze,
I feel your gentle presence and lift
my open hand toward it, toward you
Hoping for a sign, me, your first-born
who never seemed to have the time
 while you were with us still.

My hand unfolds, the monarch hovering
before it turns to float across the garden
to another bush he settles there instead.

And still I wait, wondering if it, if you,
might rise from the distant purple
and return here while I open trembling hand
and settle if only for a moment, dear woman
before you lift and travel
to some distant land as monarchs will.

How you loved butterflies.
So much so I had one etched on your gravestone
when you left us that September
having given us all you had
before the cancer took you
took you on, too soon.

Remember that final phone call

your voice already tired,
when I said I'd be there, I said, I said,
then driving north through the rain-soaked night,
getting lost, and more lost as on we drove,
and getting there too late.
Stay now, mother.
Stay just a little longer, before you're off again
bound for some other place called home.

[*audience applause*]

The next one is for my 16-year-old granddaughter, Juliana. At Christmas, she painted a portrait of her and me from an old photograph taken in Cape Cod, at the beach. There are no faces, just the outlines: the little girl that I'm holding in my arms, three years old, and her grandpa. She painted that, and when she gave it to me, I just broke down. So, I wrote a poem in response to her painting. It's called "Miss Juliana Revisited: 12 Years On."

Flat blue sky, and a seaweed sea composed of moss and myrtle trees
And two thin brushstrokes for whitecaps
In what would be the distance
And there facing you, two faceless figures
both smiling perhaps
One is a man, white cap highlights
defining his grey hair for him
shadow his only other feature
his t-shirt a monochrome of blue —
that would be you

The other is a little girl
age three or so in a lavender
two-piece bathing suit decked out with
asterisks like rose pink purple stars
a little girl so full of life
in whom he holds in both his arms
tight against his chest as if had the power
to keep her from all harm.

Somewhere he hopes a world
much like the world his granddaughter has painted
here exists. A world no one can ever tear
from them and if not that,
oh, if not that,
then at least a world where
he can always hold her in his heart.

[*audience applause*]

The next poem is called "On the Way Home." My wife Leta and I made a trip to the Canadian Rockies a year ago. It was overcast, raining like crazy, cold, snow falling in September, and then suddenly the light broke through above and it was like a transfiguration moment.

there was a moment
we were coming down
from the turbulent waters
of the Maligne it had been
raining for what seemed
hours on end there was
a thick mist hanging in the air,
a billowing high above
the larches and the pines
so that the mountain peaks
seemed all but hidden
when suddenly without warning
the face of one mountain
far off to our left began
to shine it was as if
some mystery had just revealed
the merest glimpse of what it was
I thought of Peter bartering
with Jesus on the Mount
of Transfiguration to stay, stay,
or Moses alone there on the Mountain
as the wind whispered

in all but words here I am
immerse yourself in me now,
now, for even this must pass
and you will descend, returning
to a world which will or will not
care but know too that this moment
may well return and it will be as if
we came together then for good.

[audience applause]

Thank you. There are two more. This one is a little more comical. It's called "Hornet's Nest," and it's based on a job I was doing, cleaning off the porch, when I sprayed a hornet's nest — and you know what can happen. [*audience laughter*] This poem has a little head note: "I really feel I can touch you even in this darkness when I pray." These are the words of James Foley, who was executed in 2014, and come from his last message to his family.

Recovered now enough to scrub the deck,
which turned dun brown with insidious dirt
and cobwebs in the months I twisted, hurt-
ing in yet one more hospital bed, my spine a wreck,
my wobbling brain awash in static bubbles
instead of what I used to tell myself were tough,
astringent thoughts. Oh, Lord, they say, the troubles
I've seen. Well, Jack, get over that self-pity stuff.
Your dear wife has a job for you to do,
so do it. Soap & water (warm works best),
a sponge, a piston stream of water and, Jack, you
have it! Progress! Until you spray a hidden nest
of hornets, who come at you, each a fighter plane
zigging this way, then that, to catch you by surprise
as your left wrist then your right foot erupt in pain.
And now they've found your face, and both your eyes,
and you beat what the Brits call a hasty retreat.
But dammit this is your porch, your house, your home,
and if these S.O.B.s had just remained discreet

or — better — stayed hidden in their aerodrome
you might have done the live let live. But no! Not now.
This is war, and either you or they will have to go.
And so you grab two cans of Raid and POW!
And it's right in the kisser, as Gleason would say. Hello
my pretty ones! By now I'm hornet mad myself, and keep
hitting them with everything I've got. And they hit back
with everything they've got. Worse, they have deep
reserves, as one winged fiend multiplies by twenty, Jack.
And soon you're like Cuchulain swinging at the sea
as wave on wave keeps coming in. And in the end
you know you cannot win, though you win this round. Be
there when they swarm me, You, my first, fast, last Friend.

[*audience applause*]

This final poem I wrote last year at Pentecost, Easter. Just…something happened. It was a space…a space opened for me. It's called "What Happened Then."

What Happened Then
Do we understand what happened then?
The few of us in that shuttered room,
lamps dimmed, afraid of what would happen
when they found us? The women back
this morning to tell Peter what they'd seen.
Then these two back from Emmaus.
And now here he was. Here in the room with us.
Strange meeting this, the holes there
in his hands and feet and heart.
And who could have guessed a calm like this
could touch us. But that was what we felt.
The deep relief you feel when the one
you've searched for in a crowd appears,
and your unbelieving eyes dissolve in tears.
For this is what love looks like and is
and what it does. "Peace" was what he said,

as a peace like no other pierced the gloom
and descended on the room.

Thank you. [*audience applause*]

"When I Cannot Sing My Heart, I Can Only Speak My Mind"

*A presentation by writer **John Waters** on rock and roll as a quest for the Infinite, or at least the moment when "the whatness of the song leaps to us from the vestments of its appearance"*

Introduction

The descent-into-cliché of much rock music is not the fault of the musicians, but a trick of time. And yet it alerts us to something really interesting: that pop music is a code that can confirm what we already understand and have become bored by, while also being a language that takes us deep into ourselves, to our hunger for the unknowable, the infinite and the great. It seems an extraordinary burden to place on a fragile pop song, but we all know songs that manage to carry it nonetheless, having acquired through time some mysterious alchemy that enables this combination of words and notes and sounds to alert us to the danger of confusing what we are hearing with mere attraction to a fashion expressed in sound, or to nostalgia for particular moments in our lives.

❖   ❖   ❖   ❖   ❖

Video of Elvis Presley singing "Can't Help Falling in Love."

John Waters: That was the song I wanted to start with, but I had a difficulty trying to decide which version; there are many versions of that song, particularly in the Vegas years. I have a bigger reason for playing that song, though, and that particular version really seems to me to encapsulate something of the extraordinary story and tragedy of Elvis Presley. Which

---

Saturday, February 16, 2019

115

is probably the greatest tragedy in popular music, because we don't really understand it, what it was about, why it happened. A man who had everything we think we might want in the world. Just a few years after that performance, about six years after that, he died on his toilet. And you can see the degeneration of him in that song, as he sang it. Every time, until finally, in June 1977, the last performance before he died two months later.

This talk is based upon an exhibition I gave two years ago in Rimini, Italy. Some of it will be obvious to everybody. Maybe all of it will be obvious to everybody. But I think it's not obvious to the culture, and that's why I wanted to do it. There's something more in all of this than we allow ourselves to talk about, than we allow ourselves to see. And that video, that particular song, that version — it's really extraordinary because it's Elvis at his finest, being what Elvis is. You can see in the faces of those two women who are watching him — it's not lust, it's something bigger than lust, it's beyond that. It's an attraction to something extraordinary. Elvis knows this and is privileged, and he knows he is because he was a real gentleman in his sensibility. He knows the gift he has and he sings the song, but more than that the song sings him. And this is a particular thing in rock and roll that we don't see so much or know of: the idea of a song in rock and roll is something much more than a song in any other context. Because so much depends on not just on the construction of the song, the words to meditate on, but on the personality. The song's personality of the singer. There's an Irish word called *yarraege*. It comes from a great Irish tenor called John McCormack. He invented this word as a description of the moment when the singer ceases to sing the song, and the song starts to sing the singer. And this is what we see in that video more than anything else. Elvis is being sung by the song. He's not really a singer at all; he's something more than a singer. He's Elvis; and this is really what was his tragedy, because he's in a place that nobody can reach him, and he can't reach anybody else because he has this extraordinary gift.

In the video you can actually see the tragedy. That moment when he impishly picks up the carton and peeps out, it's almost like he's a prisoner, and knows it. And he's looking out at these people he can't really be a part of anymore. And then you go back, you see from behind that he can't — he's led away like he's a prisoner. And that is the tragedy of Elvis; that he

116

achieved everything that one could want, or might think one would want. It was a gift, and yet he was a prisoner and died a prisoner just a few years later. And that's kind of what I wanted to get out of this.

When I was writing at Hot Press about music, I didn't know what to do, I didn't know what it was about until I read this extract from Greil Marcus' *Mystery Train*. Flannery O'Connor said that the novel was essentially about two things: mystery and manners. I wrote a book about U2 years ago and I said rock and roll is really about two things: mystery and mischief. And again, you can see that in the video about Elvis. Someone had told me the formula of writing about a concert. You write a review of the concert, add a little bit about the crowd, and a little bit about the band that played, where, who played what. Maybe an incident happens and you can write about that, too. In those days, everybody wrote about music pretty much the same way, with the same formula. One day I was reading this book by Greil Marcus called *Mystery Train*, about Elvis. He's a great American writer. And here's a passage in the book: "There are those moments when Elvis Presley" — he's talking about being in Vegas and watching Elvis, first time seeing him live — "breaks through the public world he has made for himself, and only a fool or a liar would deny their power. Something entirely his, driven by two decades of history and myth, all live-in-person, is transformed into an energy that is ecstatic — that is, to use the word in its old sense, illuminating. The overstated grandeur is suddenly authentic, and Elvis brings a thrill different from and far beyond anything else in our culture; like an old Phil Spector record, he matches, for an instant, the bigness, the intensity, and the unpredictability of America itself."

"It might be that time when he sings 'How Great Thou Art' with all the faith of a backwoods Jonathan Edwards; it might be at the very end of the night, when he closes his show with 'Can't Help Falling in Love,' and his song takes on a glow that might make you feel his capacity for affection is all but superhuman. Whatever it is, it will be music that excludes no one, and still passes on something valuable to everyone who is there. It is as if the America that Elvis throws away for most of his performance can be given life again at will."

I couldn't change my whole attitude towards what writing was, about what music was. Marcuse said, "His song takes on a glow that might make you feel his capacity for affection is all but superhuman." I thought, That's it! That's the bar. That's what Elvis is. But that's also the bar if you want to write about it, if you want to write about this stuff, that's the way you have to think about it. It's not about the quality of performance, it's not about the sight of entertainment, it's not even about your favorite musicians and their songs. There's something else happening. Capacity for affection is almost superhuman.

A lot of what I'm doing is just putting together quotes from people, and a few of them are from myself, because as the great Irish poet Patrick Kavanagh said, you should always tell the truth. Sometimes the Irish have better quotes than the ones I do. So, he said you should always tell the truth even when it's unfair to yourself. [*audience laughter*] Brian Eno said this: "I think the echo on Elvis' "Heartbreak Hotel" is better than the song itself, by far. Nobody could tell me what that was, in my family. They didn't know what to make of that sound. It turned the studio into a cave. When I was young, the most overpowering sense of wonder was inspired in me by music."

One of the things when we were growing up, and we loved this music was that people would complain that they couldn't make out the words, they didn't know what the words were about. And that's true, but it actually doesn't matter. The first song we adored was by an English band called T. Rex, whose singer, Marc Bolan, also came to a terrible end a very short time after Elvis. The song was called "Ride a White Swan." And to this day I still don't have a clue what the words are about. But it changed my life because when I heard the song, I thought, This is a different place now, this is a different way of seeing the world, it's a different view of the world. And it's mine, I share it. This guy knows something about me that I didn't even know about myself, even though we have never met. We have to be very careful not to overload things, because the very nature of this music is that it's modest about itself. It's evasive about itself. In the modern world, so many people are isolated within themselves and they have intuitions about things, which I don't think anybody shares. And more and more the pressure bows upon us to sit silent about lots of stuff, which means that we feel that we alone have this sense of the world. As a kid I didn't have a clue when

I heard songs that I could relate to, that I thought, "Ah, I'm not actually on my own. I'm not the only crazy person that thinks like this." I don't necessarily mean that when I use the word "transcendence" in this context, that it's necessarily — you can decide —*religious* transcendence. Or how we think of it as religious. But I think it is, nevertheless, transcendent, and in two ways. One is backwards transcendence, and the other transcendence is into the infinite future. I think this is what the music aims for. This is why we loved it. We didn't know, we thought it was just because it was hip and cool and all that. But the reason it was hip and cool and all that was because it was tuned to self, and that connected with us. But nobody told us, because when we read about it in the papers, it was always in the tabloids. These people were called "rockers," and the whole thing was completely reductive. I always felt kind of embarrassed by that. That we like this music despite the fact that it could be given this kind of description. So, it's like something was there but we never knew what it was. The song — "Ride a White Swan" — went something like this:

Ride it on out like a bird in the sky ways
Ride it on out like you were a bird
Fly it all out like an eagle in a sunbeam
Ride it on out like you were a bird"

And then the guitar solo. The amazing thing about that song is something that happens with a lot of songs: even at my age I can hear that song and be instantly transported, teleported, not to a place, but to a certain place in myself. And the only thing about that song that destroys that is the guitar solo. That's very interesting, because it's the guitar solo uniquely, alone in that song, that has been rendered cliché in the interim, because people have imitated it so much. It's become like a meme of rock and roll. Brian Eno used to warn about this, the producer who produced Talking Heads, U2, and lots of different bands — Coldplay. He called himself a non-musician even though he did play with Roxy Music, he played keyboards. He always warned about the danger of musicianship. That you couldn't be in rock and roll if you were too good, if you got to be proficient. That you were in danger all the time of turning out clichés. It's something that we can recognize in the music we hear nowadays — or maybe it's just because I'm getting old as well. [*audience laughter*] I said the descent into cliché is not the fault of the musicians but a trick of time. And yes, it alerts us to something really interesting: that music tends to confirm what we already understand and have become bored by. But it's also a language that takes us deep into ourselves, because of our hunger for the fantastic and the infinite and the great. It seems an extraordinary burden to place on a fragile pop song.

John Lennon wrote in a letter to Stuart Sutcliff, one of the original band members, "I can't remember anything without a sadness, so deep that it hardly becomes known to me." Like Elvis, extraordinarily tragic, these people. Amy Winehouse. They were tasked with the gift of singing not just their own griefs and their own joys, but ours also. And this is why we wanted to see them; this is why we wanted to hear them. We didn't necessarily think about it in those terms. I think of Amy Winehouse — I've written about her before. She was this extraordinary, fragile thing, like the filament of a bulb into which was pumped 10,000 volts of pure energy. Same was true of Elvis. Same is true of all these people. What you don't read in the tabloids is that, when you're up there and you're doing that, you're singing the heart of every person listening and watching. Where do you go? They're sitting and watching you, listening. They're moved. You're lifted up into space. You can't come back for a long time. And you do this again and again, night after night after night, and the cost of it becomes so tremendous it can never be repaid. It's a debt that runs off the page.

Paul Morley, in his book *Words and Music*, which I really suggest as probably one of the greatest music books about rock and roll that's been written, has as its thesis something like this: that the spirit of rock and roll at that moment resided not with Coldplay but with Kylie Minogue. And he actually makes the thesis sustain itself in the book. But he starts the history of rock and roll off with Big Band and then goes through the various events that led up to this. I'll just give you a few examples. We're talking about the music that started, you could say in another sense, with the slaves and the plantations. Chanting to one another, shouting out, shouts becoming chants, becoming lines of songs that became the blues. Folk and country, strands that come from Europe; from Ireland, my own country. So in the beginning there was this cry. The first cry of man was 2.8 million years ago; then this call and response, and then the first rhythm.

Jean-Jacques Rousseau said, "The first utterances were delivered by the hands of another. His bleat at the first musical instrument was for ritual not harmonious purposes." It was not hunger or thirst, he said, but love, hatred, pity and anger which drew from men their first vocal utterances.

Gregorian chant: AD 600. The metronome: 1814. In 1798, in George Colman's one act farce, *Blue Devils*, the term "the blues" first surfaces as a way of describing melancholy, sadness. In 1800, Mozart composed his Requiem Mass, and at the same moment, the blues began to develop along the Mississippi Delta, emanating from the various Christian working songs, spirituals, chants. Blues' deepest roots were in the work songs of the West African slaves in the Deep South of the U.S. To ameliorate the pain of a life of back-breaking toil in the fields of the southern plantation owners, these black slaves developed a call and response mode of singing. This formed the basis of what became known as the blues. And so on.

Nietzsche said, "For it is only through the spirit of music that we can understand the joy involved in the annihilation of the individual." When you talk about rock and roll, you are expected to accept that it's an inferior, lower form of music. That's not the case I'm making here at all. I'm actually saying that it's more than that. And these guys are certainly saying this. The reason traditional notation works is because classical music is so simple. The notes are discreet. We tend to go [*sings like a choir boy*] "Ah, ah, ah, ah ah." You don't go [*makes one guttural noise up and down*] like they do in the blues or in Arab music. That kind of thing is almost unnotable. And everything else in classical music is discontinuous. A clarinet is a clarinet, a trombone is a trombone. This isn't the case in modern music. There's everything in-between as well.

I had written a book about U2. And U2 could do no wrong. I'll come back to that. When rock and roll started out, it was not understood, and was obviously, you know, music made by idiots. Because people couldn't get this beat. It was going on in Memphis, it was one of the most extraordinary moments of the 20th century, when African rhythm and European melody were married. Two cultures collided in a spastic dance, a guy who wore eye shadow and a Zoot suit. It was an extraordinary thing, but it completely missed the intelligentsia, the people who were going to the opera, or listened to what was described as the modern music of the time. And here it was happening in Ducktown, in the back of a shop.

John Lennon said this, a beautiful quote: "The blues is real. It's not perverted, it's not thought about, it's not a concept — it's a chair. Not a design for a chair, or a better chair, or a bigger chair, or a chair with leather or with design — it's the first chair; chairs for sitting on, not chairs for looking at or being appreciated. You sit on that music."

Orchestras can't play a rhythm. The most brilliant musicians in the world and the finest orchestras, we can't get them to play a rhythm. They don't understand it. It's like a muscle they haven't developed. And rock and roll music is where Africa and Europe collide. There in that moment. Rhythm is not articulate. Jimi Hendrix said, "A musician, if he's a messenger, is like a child who hasn't been handled too many times by man, hasn't had too many fingerprints across the brain. That's why music is so much heavier than anything you ever felt."

The era; this moment; this song. This is where I think rock and roll is so different from every other form of music. The performance needs to be everything. A song written by one songwriter for one singer can maybe never match anybody else, be the most extraordinary thing, and everything else be a failure afterwards. Or the opposite sometimes happens: somebody writes a song and it's nothing, and then somebody else sings it, and it's new. There's a song by Bruce Springsteen that's like that, I think. "Highway Patrolman." He sings it okay. But then Johnny Cash sings it and it's just *epic.* He just sings it as Johnny Cash; he doesn't do anything other than be Johnny Cash. Somehow, in his voice, it's one of the greatest stories ever told.

Fr. Giussani had a wonderful phrase about words. He said: "We use the least inadequate words." It's kind of an admission that all words are a failure. Everything; all writing is a failure. You don't succeed in saying what you want to say. All you succeed in is offering a truth that somebody else will recognize and not require all the words that you've used to say it because they knew it already. Patrick Cavanaugh used to say that poetry wasn't literature, it was theology. And the quality of a poem that made it a poem was what we called the "flash," which essentially got the poem into the world. And that, he said, was the function of the poet: to make God visible in the world. There's something about the mystery of what words do in a rock and roll song, because you can hear the same song many times, you can love the song, and think you have a vague idea of what it is about, but when you see the words written down it's something completely different. It happens to me all the time, but it doesn't actually matter, because it's saying something deeper than the words. And you're attracted to that. Whatever that is.

The great singers, like Van Morrison, probably the greatest white blues singer — he's Irish, sorry. [*audience laughter*] When you listen to him, it's like he's constantly attacking the words and trying to destroy them, trying to break them up into fragments and deliver them in some way that will actually transcend themselves, escape from their literal meanings and become something that is related to the music in a way that he can't possibly explain and you can't possibly understand, and yet you gaped when you heard it. Paul Morley talks about words and music. He talks about the abstract series of sounds, shapes, and noise forms that can communicate something specific to us without the use of words. It begins in words but somehow the words are absolved into something else. Some ambition greater than the words will become beyond description and telling, via poetic devices like onomatopoeia, alliteration, and assonance. Morley says that the words in a song disappear into themselves as if boiled down, as if they are changing from solid to liquid, forming a sensuous, absorbing musical form that implies how all music began with the sound of the human voice. The sound of the human voice imitating sounds around us; the sounds of nature, animals, even the sound of silence. The sound of the human voice copying the voice of God.

Now, Paul Morley is an atheist, so we need to know what he understands is God. I shared a platform with him one time and inadvertently used the word God while I was speaking, and I think he got a bit freaked out. [*audience laughter*] But he's really an extraordinary writer, because he's one of these great writers who you feel safe with from the very first sentence. You know he's not going to lead you astray, and that he's going to lead you somewhere really special. Paul Morley's exceptional. If you can get that book, it's great. And he wrote another great book called *Nothing*, about the death and suicide of his father. It's exceptional.

John Lennon said: Why do I have to explain what sound is? I mean, we all sit by the sea and listen to it. People just lie in the fields and listen to birds, and nobody says a thing.

Language and song, he said, is from me. Apart from being true vibrations, it's like trying to describe a dream, and because we don't have telepathy or whatever it is, we try to describe the dream to each other, to verify to each other what we know, what we believe is inside each other. But no matter how you say it, it's never how you want to say it. *Yarragh* is kind of a fusion of several words — they're not quite words at all. They contain something of an exclamation: *Yarragh!* If you met somebody in the street: *Yarragh!* Or sometimes it's an expression of grief, or sometimes of joy. It's a kind of affirmation, a *yes*.

Greil Marcus said about Van Morrison: "His music can be heard as an attempt to surrender to the *yarragh*, or to make it surrender to him; to find the music it wants; to bury it; to dig it out of the ground. The *yarragh* is his version of the art that has touched him: of blues and jazz, and for that matter of Yeats and Lead Belly, the voice that strikes a note so exalted you can't believe a mere human being is responsible for it, a note so unfinished and unsatisfied, you can understand why the eternal seems to be riding on its back."

He said, "Morrison will take hold of the *yarragh*, or get close to it, raise its specter even as he falls back before it, for the moment defeated, with horns, volume, quiet, melody and rhythm and the abandonment of both, in the twist of a phrase or the dissolution of words into syllables and syllables into preverbal grunts and moans. He will pursue it perhaps most of all in repetition, railing or sailing the same sound 10, 20, 30 times, until it has taken his song where he wants it to go or failed to crack the wall around it."

And John Lennon, in a beautiful song for his mother, Julia: "When I cannot sing my heart, I can only speak my mind, Julia." Einstein and Newton, anything that was discovered was discovered by accident, by creative spurt.

What did Einstein do? He spied the theory of relativity when he was working on something else. He spent the rest of his life trying to prove something else, which you can never do. So, what he did, really, was live off of that record for the rest of his life. [*audience laughter*] Not taking away from his brilliance or natural ability, but the real creation came when he sat there and something came to him. Or when the apple fell on Newton's head. He never would have had the apple fall on his head, and conceive of what it meant, had he not been sitting under the tree daydreaming. For me, it's the same with music. Lennon again: "The real music comes to me, the music of the spheres, the music that surpasses understanding, that has not to do with me, of which I am just a channel. So, for that to come through, which is the only joy for me, the music is to be given to me and I transcribe it like a medium. But I have nothing to do with it other than I am sitting under the tree, and the whole damn thing comes down and I just put it down."

Bono said, "The way we write, sometimes we feel like the song is already there. If we can just put it into words, put it into notes, we have it but it's not realized, yet, it's not formed."

Dylan said: "I had a wife and children whom I loved more than anything else in the world. I was trying to provide for them, keep out of trouble, but the big bugs in the press kept promoting me as the mouthpiece, spokesman, or even conscience of a generation. That was funny. All I'd ever done was sing songs that were dead straight and expressed powerful new realities. I had very little in common with and knew even less about a generation that I was supposed to be the voice of. I had left my hometown only ten years earlier, I wasn't vociferating the opinions of anybody. My destiny lay down the road with whatever life invited, had nothing to do with representing any kind of civilization. Being true to myself, that was the thing. I was more a cowpuncher than a Pied Piper."

Dylan again. "We're all sinners. People seem to think that because their sins are different from other people's sins, they're not sinners. People don't like to think of themselves as sinners. It makes them feel uncomfortable. 'What do you mean sinners?' It puts them at a disadvantage in their mind. Most people walking around have this strange conception that they're born good, that they're really good people — but the world has just made a mess of their lives. I have another point of view. But it's not hard for me to identify with anybody who's on the wrong side. We're all on the wrong side, really."

And finally: "If you're talking just on a scriptural type of thing, there's no way I could write anything that would be scripturally incorrect. I mean, I'm not going to put forth ideas that aren't scripturally true. I might reverse them, or make them come out a different way, but I'm not going to say anything that's just totally wrong, that there's not a law for. The Bible runs through all U.S. life, whether people know if or not. It's the founding book. The founding fathers' book, anyway. People can't get away from it. You can't get away from it wherever you go. Those ideas were true then and they're true now. They're scriptural, spiritual laws. I guess people can read into that what they want. But if you're familiar with those concepts they'll probably find enough of them in my stuff. Because I always get back to that."

We live in a world where it's impossible to communicate really deep and complicated things that we all feel to each other in our culture. Maybe they happen in books and we can read them in private. They're not on TV. They're not on the radio. They're certainly not on Twitter. So, more and more we're isolated in this kind of moronic cacophony where we just regurgitate the slogans and mantras, the simplistic memes. And rock and roll exists — in my opinion — to be the antidote to that, and always has. But because of the nature of that culture that encloses it, it needs to conceal its true purpose. That's why you have all this confusion about what rock and roll really is. It's entertainment. And there are so many eruptions of things: narcissism, hedonism, and nihilism, which distract and give fodder to the tabloids. Amy Winehouse...she died of alcohol poisoning. No; she died of misunderstanding her genius, of underestimating what she had; of not having anybody to tell her what actually was happening to her being and her body. That's the tragedy of Elvis, that's the tragedy of all these people. There's a process by which the artist wrote this song in a hotel room, or whereever, and that song has something profound but undeniable that is communicated to all these masses of wires and signals, and then finally to the listener in his or her bedroom, through a pair of headphones. That communication is complete — and you see that's where you get the ecstatic response to rock and roll that you see in the concerts. Suddenly, all of the people come out of their bedrooms and stand in front of a person who represents this promise, almost like a ritual. Our culture doesn't allow us to talk about these things, and very rarely does anybody break the silence about it, as to the real meaning of what is actually at play. But from time to time somebody does something that alerts us to the true significance of what is happening. It's ironic that the person who did this is the artist who more and more became defined by the tabloid cliché of the degenerate lifestyle of rock and rollers. The hedonistic, the nihilistic. But then he went on another journey, and he stopped drinking and drugging and he started going to Alcoholics Anonymous. Then, about 1990-91, there was a concert celebrating the first anniversary of the death of Freddie Mercury, lead singer of Queen. There's a video on YouTube. You can find it but nobody ever mentions it. It's probably one of the most sensational moments, in my opinion, in rock and roll history but nobody ever talks about it. It's not in any book. There aren't any articles about it. But David Bowie does something in this moment that acknowledges all this, and takes us into the truth about where we are, what is happening, and why it's happening.

Video of David Bowie saying the Our Father at the Freddie Mercury tribute concert

The Education of the Heart

*Re-thinking education at the end of an epoch. With **Jon Balsbaugh**, President of the Trinity Schools Network; **Archbishop Christophe Pierre**, Apostolic Nuncio to the United States; **Stanley Hauerwas**, Professor Emeritus of Divinity and Law, Duke Divinity School (video contribution); and moderated by **Holly Peterson**, Principal of Nativity: Faith and Reason School in Broomfield, Colorado*

Introduction

"The fundamental idea in the education of the young is the fact that it is through the younger generations that society successively rebuilds itself. Therefore, the primary concern of society is to teach the young. This is the opposite of what currently happens. Our main theme in all of our writings and lectures has always been education: how to educate ourselves, what education consists of, and how it takes place. We mean a true education, one that matches human reality — that is, educating what is human in us, our source or origin. Although expressed in different ways in each individual, this properly human dimension always reflects the same substance, for behind the diversity of different cultures, customs, and expressions, the human heart is one and the same: my heart is your heart, and it is the same heart that beats in men and women who live far away in other countries or continents. The first concern of a genuine and appropriate educational method is the education of the heart of man, just as God made it, for after all, ethics is nothing more than the continuation of the attitude in which God originally created humanity in its relation to all things."

~Luigi Giussani, *The Risk of Education*, Crossroad, 2001, page 7

Sunday, February 17, 2019

❖　❖　❖　❖　❖

Holly Peterson: Good morning, everyone. This morning we have three guests with us, two present and one virtual, who will help us understand what the education of the heart is. To my far right is Jon Balsbaugh. He has over 20 years of experience as a high school and junior high teacher, and he currently serves as the President of Trinity Schools, a nationwide network of classically-oriented Christian schools. Before taking over as president, he served as a headmaster of Trinity School in River Ridge, designed Trinity Schools' poetry curriculum, and worked extensively in teacher training. Mr. Balsbaugh received his Master's degree in English from the University of Saint Thomas, studying the theological aesthetics of Hans Urs von Balthasar. He has published on C.S. Lewis and is currently serving as the editor-in-chief of *Veritas*, an online journal of education.

To my immediate right — I don't know if he needs an introduction — is Archbishop Pierre, who has been with us all weekend, which has been an amazing joy. Archbishop Christophe Pierre was born two weeks ago. [*audience laughter*] I was his birthday. He was born in France, and was ordained a priest in 1970. After having completed his studies at the Pontifical Ecclesiastical Academy in Rome, he was appointed as the Pontifical Representative of New Zealand and the Pacific Islands. Subsequently, he served in Mozambique, Zimbabwe, Cuba, Brazil, and at the Permanent Mission of the Holy See in the United Nations in Geneva. He has been appointed the Papal Nuncio in Haiti, Uganda, Mexico, and now here in the United States. He lives in Washington, D.C., and you can find more about our two speakers in the program. Our third guest is Dr. Stanley Hauerwas, Emeritus Professor of Divinity in Law at Duke's Divinity School, and we will hear his intervention first.

Video

Peterson: I'm Dr. Holly Peterson, I'm the principal of Nativity Faith and Reason School in Colorado, and I'm with Dr. Stanley Hauerwas, Professor Emeritus of Divinity and Law School here at Duke University in Durham, North Carolina. Dr. Hauerwas has written the forward for the recently published new edition of *The Risk of Education* by Fr. Luigi Giussani, the founder of Communion and Liberation. This interview is being made on the occasion of the discussion of Archbishop Christophe Pierre, Dr. Jon Balsbaugh, and all who are taking part in the New York Encounter 2019.

Dr. Hauerwas, in your forward to the new edition of *The Risk of Education*, you quote approvingly Fr. Giussani's statement, "that to educate means to help the human soul enter into their totality of the real." You also agree with his claim that "this is possible only in relationship with a person rich in awareness of reality, that is, the teacher." Giussani rightly calls into question any education that is based on the assumption that a person has total autonomy and that leaves the student fearful of confronting the world. So, what does it mean to enter into the totality of the real, and what is the role of the teacher in this regard?

Dr. Stanley Hauerwas: To enter into the totality of the real, first and foremost means you're able to see connections, and connections are a way of helping you discover that we are creatures created by God, who gives life purpose. There is no subject who does not need to be formed by the love of God for one another. It is the ability to be related to God and our brothers and sisters.

Peterson: So you also state that the assumption of autonomy in education is a result of a predominant rationalism that is prevalent in society.

Hauerwas: My way of putting that is, modernity names the time when you want to create people who believe they should have no story except the story they chose when they had no story. That's called freedom, particularly in America. Modern education, therefore, thinks its primary job is, first of all, to free students from the irrational commitments of the past. I think that ends up producing people who are consumed by cynicism. The difficulty is, of course, they didn't choose the story that they should have no story except the story they chose when they had no story, and that produces an incoherence in their lives that, I think, is extraordinarily destructive.

Peterson: Switching gears a little bit, Fr. Giussani defines the human heart as the place of the original needs and evidences that we have. What does this understanding of the heart have to do with education?

Hauerwas: I think that the appeal to the heart is a way of saying there has to be a centered self in which all that we do finally has a kind of coherence that praises God. There is a wonderful book by a shepherd in England and Green Bay, it's called *Shepherd's Life*. He's done a university degree, but he remains a shepherd. The book ends with him letting out his sheep, and it turns out that raising sheep is a very complex business. You have to be very smart and you have to learn a multitude of skills, like, looking at their teeth. He lets his sheep out at the beginning of spring in the rough country in which they have to forage, and he lays down by a spring with his sheep dogs and he looks up at the clouds and says, "This is my life. I want no other." Now: to train students to have lives they wouldn't trade anything for is the great challenge, and I think that's what Fr. Giussani is about. How to train, form lives, that you wouldn't trade. I just think that is such a challenge today, that people who become consumers of their own lives turn out not to have lives that they're happy with.

Peterson: You note in your forward to the book that "we have been created by God to desire the truth." So, should the truth be the focus of education? And if so, where do skills and values fit in?

Hauerwas: I prefer to use the language of truthfulness. I gave the commencement address at the University of Aberdeen a year ago, and I said, "Most of the time, most commencement addresses no one remembers. I don't remember. I'm going to give you advice that hopefully will give you a life that you will enjoy and feel worthy of passing on, and, therefore, it's a very simple recommendation. Don't lie; don't lie. Truth matters, but we come to truth through learning how to be in relationship to one another by being truthful, and that's not as easy as it seems, because people never lie to one another more readily than when they're married. [*audience laughter*] Because they are afraid of losing the fragile intimacy that they have. So, how to be a people in the world that have a way of life that makes it possible for telling one another the truth. I think it's a great challenge, and Fr. Giussani saw it very clearly, and he knew how to be present to students and other people in a way that we would want to know the truth coming from Giussani.

Video ends. Audience applause

Peterson: So I have a question for both of you, but we'll have Jon go first. Dr. Hauerwas notes that the education of the heart which Giussani says is the locus of our primary needs — this is the place where my "I" is, right? So, this education creates a centered self; that's what Dr. Hauerwas said. How does education cultivate the heart? How does it help the heart to flourish?

Jon Balsbaugh: You know, I think that there's a really important distinction between the centered self in the way Dr. Hauerwas is talking about it and what he warned against, and what I think it's easy to confuse that with, which is an independent self. The first, to be centered in total reality, and the second, to try and find a way to be centered entirely within yourself, autonomous, free, and unmoved. The first of those is a noble human goal. The second is probably a dangerous path to spiritual isolation. So I really think another way to ask this question would be, What can education do to help people choose that first path over the second? And I think it has to start with the aim of education. We have to have an aim of education that is what Jacque Maritain called "human awakening." Not SAT scores, not college placement, not even graduation rates and literacy, as important as those latter two are — but a human awakening to reality. Once we as educators have that aim and adopt it, there's actually a fairly simple method for carrying it out. I say "simple" because it is, but it's also one of those simple arts that takes a lifetime to master, and that is, to never give an explanation to a student unless they have first encountered the reality that you are explaining.

I'll give an example: for more years than I can remember, I taught eighth grade boys literature and composition, which meant that, in the cycle of my life, come springtime, it was my job to teach these young 13- and 14-year-old boys the fine art of poetry. And in the early years, I cannot remember what I did to introduce the topic, but I remember that it was frustrating and unproductive, and I came away thinking they have no aptitude or even instinct for poetry in the way I will appreciate it, and I'm sure they felt that. But then one year I realized, They don't even know *why* a poet would write a poem. They have not had an encounter with the world that raises that poetic urge in them. So I said, "Alright boys, get up. We're going outside." This was when I was teaching in Minnesota, and one of the things that also corresponded with the spring was the great thaw, and surprisingly, at least for someone who did not grow up on the tundra, beneath that layer of snow and ice was an almost perfectly preserved layer of fall leaves. Some of them were even still crunchy, like they had just fallen off the tree. So, I said, Alright guys, I want you to pick up a handful of those leaves. I want you to roll them around in your hand until they're nice and crushed, and then I want you to put them to your nose and inhale gently and smell that. [*audience laughter*] The first year I didn't add "gently." Later iterations I added "gently." After a moment I asked them: "Okay, where did that take you? What did it remind you of?" That smell is so pungent and so particular, and the sense of smell so connected to memory, that inevitably they went back to something in the fall. A very particular event, maybe a hay barn on their uncle's farm, or a freshly-mown alfalfa field, something in the fall. And I said, "Okay, look around: the buds are on the trees, the birds have come back, the grass is greening, but you hold in your hand a memory of the fall. What do you make of that?" Then we went back inside and talked about spring and fall, and what it meant, and what they felt like, and put some nouns and adjectives up on the board, and we wrote a little poem together. Then at the end of that exercise, I could tell them, Okay, that's all that poetry is about. A poet goes out into the world, encounters it with his or her senses, and then derives some sort of meaning or understanding from it and attempts to communicate it. And that really is a fairly simple method, but it provided a better introduction to poetry than anything I could have written on the board, any introduction they could have read in a textbook. This method never explains something before a student has encountered it, and it doesn't apply just to poetry. You can apply it to science, to art, even to mathematics. I was talking with another educator here earlier this week, and his approach was: every chemistry class should start by burning something. [*audience laughter*] So that's the similar instinct, and I think when you do that with students you position them to be more centered in the world, in the world of things, and in the world of people, and you give them a chance to avoid that kind of isolation or radical independence.

Peterson: Yes, thank you. Archbishop?

Archbishop Christophe Pierre: Yes. The heart. What is the heart? It's difficult, actually; we have to be careful about words and what we mean. I remember that some years ago I had a nephew taking a philosophy class. He had a dissertation to make, and it was about Descartes. Imagine: to begin philosophy with Descartes. I never understood Descartes myself, and so I told him, "That's interesting. Let's see how you begin that, because you need to have a method, an approach." And he said nothing. Later, not surprisingly, he was overwhelmed by the amount of information he was forced to digest. This is the kind of education most young people have today. We need immediate answers, and we are not prepared to receive these answers because we have no questions.

When I was about fourteen, my father was working in the southern part of Morocco, so I changed schools. That was a public school, so we had a chaplain in the school, and the chaplain one day organized a kind of retreat. I remember that at the beginning of the retreat, the chaplain — I think he was a Franciscan, and his name was, coincidentally, Fr. Christopher. He said, Today we will discover, we will tell you about who God is. When I heard that, there was a kind of blossoming of joy in my heart. I said, Finally! I will know who God is! [*audience laughter*] I don't remember anything about the answer, but I still remember today that he asked questions. The questions remained. I think this is precisely the education of the heart. This is one of the things you read when you read Giussani — I hope you know about Giussani. He always said you cannot have an answer if you don't have the right questions. For me, the questions that were put in my heart have been the beginning of a new life, in a way, because I was not ready for the answer, but it was there in preparation. This is one thing I think is very important. If you want to have a good definition about what is the heart, and the education of the heart, I think the best example is Mary, because something happened to Mary when she was approached by the angel. She was approached by God and was given a question. The first answer was not an intellectual answer, but was a simple yes. You read in the gospel: Mary kept all these things in the heart. The heart, of course, is the center of the personality. "Who am I?" Education is that. I remember when I was in Uganda, I used to be the chaplain of a movement of young adults, and we would invite people to a two- or three-day retreat. During these days, members of the movement were animated, but offering something new. New questions, new information to their friends who were then invited.

So maybe you had 50 people organizing the retreat and 15 new members invited to the retreat. During the first two days, we were giving a lot of information, a lot of questions, and I used to spend the last day, Sunday, listening, and offering the Sacrament of Reconciliation. My experience was amazing. Amazing because these two days had been the time of asking questions, and now the Sacrament of Reconciliation was a kind of answer. I think I realized how much these young people had been educated by an encounter with Christ. For example, so many young women had been through the very traumatic process of abortion. Once you realize that, you open your eyes, and your heart is helping you to make the judgment but also to make decisions. I think this is what education is all about.

I will offer another example, because I think we really need to see how it works in our own life, so that we may communicate with others, and because this is what education is all about, by the way. We need our parents: the father and mother are the first indicators, facilitators who help you discover who you are. The master — I actually prefer the word "master" to "professor" — is the best there is: he or she is the person who actually helps the person to connect his own heart with the reality where he lives. You also need someone to connect you with your background, your history. Not only your personal history, but the history of your family, the history of your culture, the history of your country. We need to be connected with our environment, and to realize that we are invited to go from the place where we are.

Peterson: Beautiful. Dr. Hauerwas said that we have no story in the modern mentality; our story has been wiped out. We have alienated our story in the name of a false sense of freedom, and that this disconnect between us and our history is ultimately a disconnect between us and God. Can you help us understand how our story is valued in knowing not only our heart, but also in knowing God?

Pierre: This is something that is helping us to understand the risk of education. There is no education if we are not introduced to reality. If we introduce reality in order to dominate it, to use it, to exploit it, then we really don't know reality. Thus we need to be introduced to reality by somebody.

Peterson: So what's our personal history have to do with our heart?

Pierre: We are not born out of nothing. We come from somebody. Our life is a gift. Everything we are is actually given to us, and I think the real education is to help us understand what we are, what we are supposed to be, what we are supposed to do. I have to receive it from somebody, and this is why I think we need to be helped by somebody who is a witness. I remember one day we had a kind of family meeting. I was about 13 or 14, and my grandparents had invited all the uncles and so forth. One of the uncles was an army man, a First Captain or something like that. He was a fat man and very talkative. At that time in France you had compulsory military service. All young men were supposed to go into the army; I did myself. "What I'm doing," he said, "is educating the young men who come into the army, and it's a very interesting job. What I do, I ask them if they have any ideal in life." What is the meaning of that? We were 13, 14. "And by the way, you young children: What is your ideal in life?" We didn't what to say; we were intimidated. Nobody answered. Later, after the party, we went home in the car. My father was driving, my mother on the side, and the six children in the backseat. It was incredible. And my father was very unhappy with that. He said, "This man, ack!" He was very nervous. He said, "These kinds of strange questions — what do you mean, What is the ideal? It's God!" Oh my God, I thought to myself. Why did I not answer that question? That was interesting, because there was somebody who was, for me, a witness. My father. And I knew that his life corresponded to his words, and he was able to tell me, to tell us, the kind of answer we should have given. This is education. Education is a kind of transmission of something. I was not able to do something, but he helped me make a connection between a question and an aspect of reality. He opened a window. When we look at our own life, we realize that what we actually have learned is not so much what we learned in books, but through witnesses.

Peterson: Thank you. Beautiful. We will give you a rest. Jon, you're on. I have a question for you now. Jon writes frequently about the word "wonder," what wonder is. How does the experience of wonder help us grow, help our heart to grow and to flourish? How does wonder in front of reality — as you just described with the leaves — generate us instead of consuming us?

How does wonder really generate our heart?

Balsbaugh: I should probably say a little something here about what we mean by "wonder." In typical speech, we tend to think of something like driving to the Grand Canyon, or going up to the Alps and having an encounter with the sublime, and in our souls it sort of resonates with that. But then it's over and we go home. Those experiences are very important to the human condition. They can refresh or even ennoble us. But what the ancients meant by wonder was something a little different. Aristotle, Plato, the others, when they talked about wonder or *thaumazein*, they were talking about something that was intrinsically generative; it led immediately somewhere. Wonder for them was actually more like a deep curiosity or perplexity, or even a kind of uncomfortable befuddlement. So in the moment of wonder they recognized that they were ignorant, and needed to learn and to move forward and encounter reality more deeply and more fully. They may not have put it exactly this way, but I think in those moments of wonder we also start a dialogue with the world, like, if you think about those boys with the leaves in their hands, they were beginning a poetic dialogue with the world.

Now what does that have to do with the education of the heart? There's a great line from T.H. White's Arthurian novel, *The Once and Future King* — which is a great book on education by the way. In it, Merlin the wizard is trying to console Arthur, his protege and young student at the time, in a moment of darkness for him. And he says the best thing for sadness is to learn something; that is the one thing that never fails. Now if we were just talking about the academic life I would absolutely disagree. If somebody comes up to me and says, "I'm sad," then I'm not going to tell them to sit in a classroom for eight hours. [*audience laughter*] That's unproductive. But if we connect this experience to wonder, to an investigation in the world and a dialogue with the world, I think Merlin may really be on to something there. Because when we wonder, when we encounter that moment of confusion, even, or curiosity, the world is suddenly not a neat and tidy and self-contained place. Not all sadness is bad, and not all sadness is the same, but there is a kind of sadness that comes from being disconnected from the things of the world. I think it has something to do with what David Brooks was talking about last night with *acedia*, or what the earlier panel was talking about in terms of loneliness. This notion of things simply being boring is wrapped up in that, so maybe this is a particular kind of sadness that wonder can help address, because when we wonder, the world suddenly becomes a different place than it was five minutes ago. It's more open; we make some contact with mystery, and every moment of wonder seems to bring with it a kind of awareness of the freshness and vitality of the world as it was when we were children. And that can't help, I think, but nourish our heart and center us in a certain way.

I'll say one other thing for wonder and that is its connection to friendship. C.S. Lewis wrote in *The Four Loves* what it takes to make a transition from being near-companions to being genuine friends, and he said that that happened when two or more people realized that something deep in their heart, either a unique delight or a unique burden, was shared by another person. So the actual moment of friendship began when two or more people said, "What? You too? I thought I was the only one." And I think, even in a formal academic environment, those moments of wonder that you can experience in a classroom sow the seeds for friendship. Maybe at first the classroom, or a little group of friends, becomes a community of learners; but eventually that becomes community in another way as well. Some of my former students were here, and I wanted to make sure this was true, so I asked them. I said, "Is this your experience of wonder?" Because we speak that language in our school. "Did it make you better friends?" And they paused for a moment and said, "Yeah, absolutely. We became friends through those kinds of encounters." Somewhat comically, they also reminded me that there's a flip-side to this. In a burgeoning friendship or relationship, if you suddenly find out that that person does not share a delight for something that is dear to you, it almost becomes an obstacle to friendship. So, if I find out somebody absolutely hates Bob Dylan, I'm not sure we can continue here. [*audience laughter*] Like, where can we go from *that* ground? But at any rate, experiences of wonder shape the soul in a certain nourishing way, and lay the seeds for friendship that really does address this fundamental loneliness and boredom.

Peterson: I have just a follow-up question to that. The archbishop just talked about the importance of a witness. What's the role of the teacher in evoking this wonder? And what about the role of the teacher as a witness?

How does a teacher grow in wonder?

Balsbaugh: Well, I think a teacher absolutely has to be, above all else, a witness to these things. I mean, the teacher has to bear witness to a love of the world, and a particular love of not just their subject, because frankly nobody really should love a subject. Your love should be directed to the reality that lies beneath the subject. I really don't think anyone should love teaching chemistry, but they should love chemical interactions and then wish to share that love with other people. The act of bearing witness is, I think, just pretty fundamental to being a teacher, and more important than any technique.

Peterson: Okay, the last question is for both of you. Dr. Hauerwas noted that he agreed with Fr. Giussani that education is about learning, leading us towards the truth, the truth of reality and of ourselves, to be happy and aware with the life that we are given. At the end he said that our task is to form lives such that we would want no other. How do educators, parents, teachers — how do we help those around us to want no other life than that which they've been given?

Balsbaugh: I think that's just such a good question, and such a good point Dr. Hauerwas made, because at the bottom it's a human question. It's there in the stories of Adam and Eve, and Cain and Abel, and Abraham and Lot, and it seems to be with us really from the cradle to the grave. How do I want the life that I have and not another? And on the other hand, it does seem to be that this is something of an urgent question in our time. It does seem that some of these things we're talking about this weekend — education at the end of an epoch; how to find something to start from — is at least wrapped up in the question of how to love the lives that we have. This does seem particularly acute for our young people and for the next generation who have inherited whatever it is that we've passed on to them. I think education, even formal education, does have a role to play, and some of the things we've talked about this morning — having a sense of your story, having a sense of being connected, having a sense of wonder in the world and developing friendships — I think those do make you like your life a little better than you otherwise would. But the last thing I would add is, there has to come a time in the education of the heart when the heart turns outward and develops a habit of active love. One of my favorite poems is "Love Calls Us to the Things of This World" by Richard Wilbur, an American poet. In the poem, the poet is in Rome and wakes up in the morning to the cry of pulleys and the laundry being put up on the wash. He looks out the window and sees the blouses and the bedsheets and the smocks passing by, and for a moment he mistakes them for angels, for celestial beings, and he has a moment of rapture. Then, as always happens in these moments, reality begins to come back in rather quickly, and he remembers his embodied existence. He remembers everything he has to do that day, and as the poem says, his soul cries out: "Oh, let there be nothing on earth but laundry, / Nothing but rosy hands in the rising steam and / Clear dances done in the sight of heaven."

I think we've all been there. We've had those transcendent experiences, and maybe for some, this weekend is one of those. Let there be nothing on earth but jazz, and poetry, and discussions, and the constant buzz of Italian conversation. [*audience laughter*] Maybe for some of us it is that kind of moment, and in a certain sense I think these moments are great, because they may be a recognition that we all long for a time when all will be well. But there is another side of it that's a little darker. If we cannot accept being brought back to the waking world, ordinary life, and the duties in front of us — I want to read the end of the poem. This comes right after the business about the cry that there would be pulleys, nothing on earth but laundry:

Yet, as the sun acknowledges
With a warm look the world's hunks and colors,
The soul descends once more in bitter love
To accept the waking body, saying now
In a changed voice as the man yawns and rises,
 "Bring them down from their ruddy gallows;
Let there be clean linen for the backs of thieves;
Let lovers go fresh and sweet to be undone,
And the heaviest nuns walk in a pure floating
Of dark habits,
 keeping their difficult balance."

I've always admired that poem and thought it had something to do with living well. As I was reflecting on it this weekend, I also realize it had something to do with educating well, because if we're going to educate the heart, there is a kind of difficult balance to be kept. The first part that Dr. Hauerwas alluded to is honesty; the first part of the balance is getting everything in and being honest about it. Thieves, lovers, and nuns in the world of the poem; all of the characters in the Bob Dylan songs, or anybody who's lost in the cosmos; and then all the ordinary people we know who are infinitely interesting but also have both good and evil in their heart; saints and sinners. We've got to get it all in and be honest with students about all of those dimensions of reality, because if we're not, they simply won't believe us if we just give them the light and don't talk to them about the darkness. They will know we're not being honest with them and they won't listen to us. But on the other side, the other part of this difficult balance is love. Love in the face of honest reality. How do we come to say, "Let there be clean linen for the backs of thieves?" To show up here this weekend and see the work of APAC [*he references here a film screened on the opening night of the Encounter, a documentary about APAC, a network of restorative justice prisons in Brazil*] was just very powerful. As educators, we have to help them keep that difficult balance.

If we can aim for human awakening, and embrace some of these simple methods — never explain anything before you encounter it, for example — and can bear witness to our students that we love the world, we love the reality beneath our subjects, we love *them*, and that ultimately the love of God surrounds everything, then education can be a powerful something to start from.

Peterson: Thank you. Archbishop?

Pierre: I was inspired by what you said. I remember the sentence of Giussani: "Education is introduction to the totality of reality." What do we mean by "totality of reality"? Are we able to embrace all of reality? The dream of many people today in our world is to embrace the total reality after having limited it. *We* want to decide what the total reality is. Real education is an introduction to reality in view of its totality. There is a different conception of the truth: truth is not something that is processed, truth is something that you are looking at. One of the problems we have even in our Church today — and some may find this controversial — is that some people insist the Church should address truth in this manner: "This is the truth, and you need to stick to it." But this is not what the Church is all about. The truth is a Person, and the only truth is the Person who said, "I am the Truth, and if you love me, you will follow me, and you will find the truth." It's a different conception, and I think the whole concept of education is like that.

Peterson: Thank you both so much for helping us with this topic, and our thanks as well to Dr. Hauerwas.

"I Just Happen to Love Ordinary Things"

A presentation by **Francis Greene**, *Art Historian, on Andy Warhol's realism and the religious sense*

Introduction

"Art is the image of creation, but if it were only this, it wouldn't have life. Art lives because it is the image of God in creation. It is the image of the return of creation to God, but art would not be alive as an image of God if the artist was not himself an image of God-Person."

~William Congdon, Notes from a talk to ISTRA, June 12, 1975

❖ ❖ ❖ ❖ ❖

Francis Greene: I'm pleased to be able to share some thoughts with you this afternoon on Andy Warhol. For those of you who may not have attended it, there is an excellent exhibition going on right now at the Whitney Museum of Art, which will continue till the end of March, on Andy Warhol's work. I highly recommend it. It's the most complete exhibition ever done, and there hasn't been a complete one on this level in over 20 years, so it's something I can highly recommend at the Whitney. In any event, Andy Warhol's life: born in 1929 and died in 1987. He was born Andrew Warhola to a Slovakian family. He changed his name, not because he was trying to disengage himself from his cultural background, but because, when he came to New York as a commercial artist, everything that was published about him repeatedly left the "a" off. Finally, he got a break with a rather major article in the *New York Times*, and they left the "a" off, too, which was

---

Sunday, February 17, 2019

really a major editing mistake. At that point he simply dropped the "a" and became known as Andy Warhol. He was born in Pittsburgh to a religious family of the Ruthenian Byzantine Church in union with Rome, and he later attended the Carnegie Institute of Technology, where his professors remember him as, first of all, very inventive, a genius in terms of ideas, and very creative ideas, but also having a superb hand for draftsmanship and line, which led to his career as a commercial designer when he came to New York in the late 1940s. He mainly created designs for the sale of shoes, but sometimes would create very avant-garde models that sometimes were adapted for shoes that were actually made. He established a very good career for himself, a good reputation as a commercial designer, and we see here some examples of them. He also did a number of store windows in major department stores, particularly Bonwit Teller, an exclusive women's department store just a few doors down from Saint Patrick's Cathedral. The building is long since gone. And this is an example of the late '40s store windows that he did. He had a reasonably good reputation. I will just say that if you look at these, they were very avant-garde, and if you look at what he did, they're not typical store windows. You see several things. In the comic strip images, you actually see a prefiguration of what would become pop art, even though it wasn't Warhol who continued the use of the comic image in pop art, but rather Roy Lichtenstein. The other thing is — and we won't have time to do it — if you went through the images, there's a gentle critique of the whole commercial enterprise. There's a sort of a gentle mocking of the very products that are being sold. Bonwit Teller understood it and they thought it was just wonderful, as did the public. But I will come back to that, this idea of a critique of the commercial world in which he was totally a part. He also designed, for a number of years, Christmas cards for major department stores and particularly for Tiffany's. We see here some of his designs.

There's the man himself. We come to 1962 and the Campbell Soup cans. After establishing his reputation, he began to paint. But he began not only to paint — which he had been doing — but to offer these for exhibition in galleries. More avant-garde galleries would be willing to accept them and put them around. He used to have ice cream regularly at Serendipity, and some of his first art that was exhibited for sale was on the walls of an ice cream shop. A high-end ice cream shop, but basically that. He began to be noticed. This is one of his Campbell Soup cans of 1962, acrylic paint on canvas. So ordinary. Every kitchen closet in those days had at least one can of Campbell's Soup. Not a very good soup in those days, it was way too salty, but everybody kept it for a rainy day. Really, a truly American product, Campbell's Soup. Suddenly, not in your cabinet but on the wall of a gallery, with gigantic proportions and in acrylic paint — a can of soup: Campbell's Soup. What are we supposed to make of it? It was really shocking to the art world; they had never seen anything like this. I want to give you a sense, a summary of the stages that the critical art world went through in dealing with Warhol. First, they ignored it. Totally. Nothing was written about it when he did his Campbell's Soup cans, Brillo boxes, and Coca-Cola. But they began to be exhibited more and more, and were beginning to be purchased by serious collectors, though rarely acquired by a museum. When they could no longer ignore him, they derided him, they laughed at this art. The critics said, "This is a man with no imagination. How little imagination could you have to paint a can of soup?" "The project is ridiculous; Coca-Cola bottles. This is somebody who's bankrupt in terms of ideas." When they could no longer deride him because increasingly he was imposing himself upon the public art world, they turned to attack. "This is bad art." I will come back to why he was attacked so viciously. Finally, when the number of collectors and galleries quietly buying his art could no longer be ignored, because he was now an international figure, these same critics then worshiped at his feet. And of course, the last stage was the worst of all, because it was the most dishonest; they were not going to be left off the bandwagon. I'll be coming back to this — the issue of his reception by the art world. This was an artist who, from the beginning, even though he ended up being the ultimate figure of the art world of his time, was really at the fringes of the outside. He had gone too far. It was okay for Andy Warhol to be a successful, American commercial designer, but to think that you're going to create paintings, acrylic paintings and silk screens, and have them exhibited in galleries and bought by important collectors — no, you've gone a little bit too far. But the fact is, he was taking a new look at very ordinary and familiar objects. In addition, in taking your can of Campbell Soup from the closet and painting an enormous canvas that could be seen on the walls of an apartment, or a gallery or museum, he was manipulating it: now it was a *painted* can of soup. He was manipulating the image; it was out of its place. What do we make of it? Now there's definitely in all of this a commercial aspect, because Warhol was a commercial designer *par excellence*. From the beginning, he had an incredibly commercial sense of how to manipulate his career, and this was one of the things he was criticized for: an artist was supposed to be poor, starving, and living in a garret. He had the ability to promote himself phenomenally, and brought a commercial sense to it. Even more relevant are the Coca-Cola bottles. My favorite is this one from 1962: green Coca-Cola bottles. Everything I just said about the soup cans could be said about the Coca-Cola bottles. It is the perfect American object. When I began teaching art in 1968, I would do a survey and would end by saying, "Class, you are looking at America today, and most people don't like what they see. When we look in the mirror and we don't like what we see, we either have to walk away from it or break the mirror." The image was somewhat painful, so it was easier to attack it or deride it. Why do I say that? If the world goes on another 100,000 years and they eventually excavate under what was once America, they are going to find more of these things in the ground than any other product you can think of. And as they have lost track of who we are, they are going to wonder, Did they worship it? What was it? [*audience laughter*] It's the ultimate American product. When China was opened under Nixon to trade and so forth, the first company that got a foothold there was a Coca-Cola bottling company. It's the ultimate American product. Every American military secret has been stolen by someone, but no one's ever gotten the formula for Coca-Cola. [*audience laughter*]

Warhol understood this. He puts it before us and stacks it up. He says, "America, here we are." And it's painful. Mass-produced — this is it. Commercial to a fault. There is a certain genius in this. Why do you paint Coca-Cola bottles? Why do you paint soup? "I just like ordinary things." And we're looking at it. From the first time I began to see it, look at it, maybe in 1966 or so, I understood it; I understood what it was about. And not because I'm a genius but because if you didn't bring baggage against him, it was so clear what he was doing. There is a gentle, gentle critique of this commercial culture from someone inside it. And the reason it's gentle and he has a right to do it is he was a shopaholic *par excellence*, he was a commercial artist, he turned this kind of art into a commercial success. So, he was trapped in this culture, and had a right to critique it, not from a moral superiority but from an experience of it.

The only time I met Andy Warhol, he was involved with ordinary things. There was, in the '70s and '80s, somewhere in Chelsea, a gigantic flea market that used to run on the weekends in some big vacant lot where they eventually put up a skyscraper. I'd always heard about it, and I like flea markets because I collect old photos. In those days you could get a beautiful *carte de visite* or cabinet card, museum quality, for two or three dollars, so if I saw those junky flea markets I would look. And one day I was cutting from a luncheon down to the F train, and I came upon a flea market I had always heard about: the Chelsea Market. Not the one we have today. I went in there. Hundreds and hundreds of tables with junk on it, okay? People milling around, and I'm looking at this long table with people on both sides looking at junk, and the next thing I know, Andy Warhol is standing there right next to me, looking at the same junk as I am. [*audience laughter*] And I remember thinking, "Oh, that's right, he collects junk. He loves to go to the flea markets." Cookie jars. He used to collect those big 1950s cookie jars, those bizarre things: they'd be, like, a clown, you could take the head off. [*audience laughter*] Or a bunch of bananas that you could take the top off of. It's said that after he died, there were shopping bags in his closets filled with them that had never been unwrapped.

So there he was, and I did what every good New Yorker would do — I ignored him totally. [*audience laughter*] Because we New Yorkers, we let our public figures go out and have a day out for themselves. I wasn't about to say, "Oh, Mr. Warhol," or whatever. And you know something? So did everybody else, because there were people on the other side of the table facing him, and nobody paid him the least bit of attention — because we were all New Yorkers. But what a quintessential moment to see him, because he loved ordinary things and this is what he understood.

Now — the attacks. Why was this art attacked? Well, it was attacked because, from the critic's point of view, he had reintroduced image into painting, in a world in which abstract painting had grown dominant. I love abstract painting, by the way, and image really was only for third-class artists in the '40s, '50s, and '60s. Warhol reintroduced images. The shock of seeing a can of Campbell's Soup painted to perfection, or Coca-Cola bottles… Forget the commercial aspect — it was a challenge to the art establishment that had been dominant for 40 years, and they went after him tooth and nail, because they rightly understood that if this art began to be accepted, then the image would return and their little tyranny of abstract and non-objective art would be over. And indeed they were right to attack it, because Andy Warhol is one of two people responsible for this change.

I want to show you very briefly the art that dominated before the Coke bottles and the soup cans. Helen Frankenthaler — this is beautiful art. Helen Frankenthaler's paintings, Jackson Pollock's extraordinary paintings — none of them with images — and most of all, Barnett Newman's *Vir Heroicus Sublimus*, the color field paintings, where basically you have one color. This was the dominant art, and a beautiful art, but it was a tyranny. When you went to art school in those days, they wouldn't teach you drawing. If you wanted to design and so forth, you were in trouble. He broke into that world with images, and that was one of the reasons he was so viciously attacked. He's one of two people who brought that about.

But he didn't just paint objects, he painted people. Such as the famous paintings of Marilyn Monroe, of which we see just one here. Ordinary people. You might say Marilyn Monroe's not an ordinary person. Mao Tse Tung, Richard Nixon, Jackie Kennedy. But they *were* ordinary people, because he saw them all every day in photographs, on TV, and in film. He takes someone ordinary, and presents them to us in a new format and asks, "Have you ever really looked?" Now for these he uses silk screen, an ancient and very old technique, centuries old, which he brought to a higher level. In the silk screen, what you do is project the image onto the support — whether it's a canvas, linen, or composite board — but then on the silk screen you filter in inks. And for each of the colors you see, you have a different stencil: you block everything out except the yellow hair, then you put on another stencil and you block everything out except the lips, and you keep adding the colors. It's a very work-intensive process that enables a kind of coloring in the images that you don't get usually with engravings and other color reproductions. Very complex. By the way, silk used to be used, but now it's either nylon or synthetic fabric. Very, very complicated. We can say without question that silk screen was brought to a level of perfection under the direction of Andy Warhol that it had never had before. Thus we have images like this one of Marilyn Monroe, a new look at a familiar image, okay? In the multiple images of Marilyn Monroe, each one is a little bit different, so the same question is asked, "Have we ever really looked at Marilyn Monroe at all?"

What are we to make of this image? What he's doing in manipulating the colors like this, is he's doing something that Marcel Duchamp, the French-American New York painter, had done in the 1920s, when he purchased a very good quality poster of the *Mona Lisa* and painted a mustache on her: he signed his initials at the bottom, framed it, then took it to a gallery. The manipulation of an iconic image. In this case, Warhol took it from a photo but reworked the colors. He's also engaging the history of Western art since the late 1870s. What happens if we take an image we've always seen and we manipulate it slightly? That's what Marcel Duchamp did with the *Mona Lisa*, way back. What happens if we rework an iconic image? Did we ever really look at Marilyn Monroe before? Have we ever really looked at our Campbell's Soup? Do you ever look, really, at a bottle of Coca-Cola? What he does is shock us into a new way of looking at ordinary things, and thus at reality. The multiple series of images, in which each one is slightly different, does something else, too: he engages what we call the question of seriality. What happens if you take not one Marilyn Monroe but nine? Or, as in one of his later paintings, 60 *Last Suppers* on a wall? Do you cheapen the image by multiplying it? What do you make of that? This is what we call seriality. What he's engaging is something that emerged in the late 19th century as a question and then disappeared. First of all, Monet. We all know Monet and those beautiful paintings of the Rouen cathedral, of which he did 32 versions of the same facade. Thirty-two versions, oil paintings. And he did so because, as you know in his art, he was focusing a different light on it, every five to 10 minutes. You're not painting the cathedral, you're painting the light, and you could easily paint 32 times. But some critics in the late 1800s said, "We're not comfortable with 32 versions of a painting. Doesn't that cheapen it?" They began to raise the question and then it died away. Or Auguste Rodin, who made of course his famous *Thinker*. But then he did about 18 other copies in stone, wood, plaster, marble, large, small, for indoors, for outdoors — a sculptor had never made so many copies of his own masterpiece. Critics were raising the question: Is this seemly? Is this something an artist should do, multiple copies? Warhol reengages all of this.

The art of Andy Warhol is, I think, very beautiful. I think the soup cans are beautiful. But more than an art of beauty, it's an art of ideas. He's constantly engaging the history of Western art at least from 1874. And this is what has to be understood as one approaches his art, which was so often reduced to cheap commercialism from men who had no imagination. Nothing could have been farther from the truth. I would recommend, by the way, the critic Rosalind Krauss, who devoted her critical life to this issue of the original and its copy. That's a work I recommend to you: Rosalind Krauss. She engages all of that.

Now, let me just summarize. He returns the image to painting, which is one of the major contributions to art that we have today, and it infuriated the entire art establishment. He raises the issue of an iconic image, something we know, manipulated as Marcel Duchamp had done. He deals with seriality, as had Monet and Rodin: the whole idea of the original and its multiple. I do want to mention before I move on to the next section, that there was one other artist who also helped reintroduce the image into American art, and that's Jasper Johns, who studied at the Parsons School of Design. You may know his American flag paintings, of which this is an example. It would be unfair not to mention him, because with Warhol, these two figures stood against the tyranny of abstract painting. I love abstract painting, but there is a place for the image as well. The thing about his paintings of flags is: they are objects also, so one critic standing in front of Jasper Johns' painting of the flag said, "I don't know if I should just appreciate it or salute it." [*audience laughter*] He got the point. The image and the object is returning.

Also, Andy Warhol is credited for being the founder of pop art: art from the popular culture, from the art of the people. Well, absolutely. Soup cans and Coca-Cola — it doesn't get much more popular than that. But that interests me the least. Yes, that's fine, great. But when you focus on that, you're missing the real contributions that this man made to American art.

I wanted to give all that as background in order to discuss with you today the religious art of Andy Warhol. Consider this photo of Warhol's studio, featuring his *Last Supper* canvas in progress. In February of 1987, Andy Warhol went in for a gall bladder operation and died overnight. This should not have happened in one of the city's best hospitals; it was totally unexpected. When his funeral took place, they exhibited this photo. In his studio, there were enormous religious paintings that almost nobody knew anything about. The critic Jane Dillenberger, who was both an art historian and a theologian in California, said, "I'm going to learn more about these." She went around, trying to find out how many religious paintings there were. And she found almost nothing. Well, it turned out there were almost 270 religious paintings, but she had the hardest time finding them. They were either owned privately, or were in galleries not being exhibited. There is the whole question of how he could have painted 112 versions of *The Last Supper*, and over 200 paintings of Christ, in the last two years of his life — but when this photo appeared at his funeral, nobody knew anything about them. Very, very interesting.

It's true that many people today who understand Andy Warhol and like his art are nevertheless surprised to hear that he had an enormous body of religious painting. As I ment ioned, his family were Ruthenian Catholics. When they couldn't worship in their own rite, they worshipped in Latin Rite parishes because the Ruthenian Church is in union with Rome — an autonomous church in full union with Rome. Now we can see him and this other side of his life. We know Andy Warhol of the Factory, Andy Warhol of all of *that* culture; but there was also the practicing, religious, believing Andy Warhol. He went to Mass almost every day, three times a week at the very minimum, as well as Sunday Mass. He wore a cross, carried a rosary, and served often at the soup kitchen of the Church of the Heavenly Rest in Manhattan, where you can check the photos of him. The people absolutely adored him, the way he took care of the homeless people — he came, waited on them, sat with them, talked with them. He financed his nephew's studies to the priesthood, but none of this is reported or discussed, ever, ever, ever. He went to St. Vincent Ferrer three times a week, and nobody said anything about him — the parishioners out of respect for his privacy and the priest out of respect — but after he died, word got out, and everybody admitted it: yes, he was there all the time.

In 1987, he created over a hundred paintings based on *The Last Supper*. I'm just going to show you a little bit of his religious art, but I want to point something out. There's this other side to Andy Warhol — the believer, the practitioner of the faith. I'm going to begin with St. Apollonia, but we have images going back to 1957, sketches. I wasn't able to get an image online of his own hand holding a beautiful, small, carved German creche. His religious art goes way back to his teen years, and certainly to his years at the Carnegie Institute of Technology. For example, in 1984 he does a whole series, seriograph on paper, of saints of the Catholic Church, including St. Apollonia. And he's basing himself, of course, on Piero Della Francesca. What he's doing in many of these is taking a saint and adapting it from a great Renaissance masterpiece, but with great respect. If you know the style of Piero, there's this kind of rigid standing, but she's holding her tooth because that's the symbol of St. Apollonia, who was tortured by having her teeth removed. These images are religious and devout, and the coloration is that of the icon in the back. He's working off earlier art in the Renaissance, but creating works that are respectful and could be exhibited in a Church and prayed in front of. There were the cross paintings of 1980, which look a little blurred but they're not. It's not that the image is badly received; I love the yellow one. And while they float forward, you see this incredible shadowing on the right side. There's a whole series of these. Again, the seriality appears.

These works were exhibited throughout Europe, but particularly in Italy, and went utterly unreported in the United States. No media carried the news of it. His large yellow *Last Suppers* were exhibited in a palazzo directly across the street from the original *Last Supper* in Milan. I want to look at a 1986 *Last Supper*, synthetic polymer on canvas, which is my favorite. The first reaction when some see this is: it's a sacrilege. You take a reproduction, in a sense, of *The Last Supper,* and you put these cheap commercial paints across it, and deface it. But nothing could be farther from the truth. First of all, he's taken *The Last Supper*, which was way up, elevated, and brought it down to our level. For the first time, you look at *The Last Supper* at its own level, which was impossible the way Leonardo created it. Secondly, the figures are larger than they were in the Milan painting. Third, he eliminates much that's distracting — the walls and so forth — and he abandons silk screen and begins to paint these by hand, on canvas and on linen, himself returning to the painted image. And suddenly we have Christ in front of us.

Next, what source does he use for the image? He uses an 1800s encyclopedia of artists, painters, and paintings, which in the 19th century was one of the major sources for critics who wrote about works of art. Many scholars who wrote about *The Last Supper* never actually saw *The Last Supper*; they used this encyclopedia. He takes this image, about which countless essays were written for over a century. Warhol raises another question: Who has ever seen *The Last Supper*? *The Last Supper* had deteriorated within its first 50 years to such a degree that, really, no one after the first 50 years has ever seen the original *Last Supper*. The fact that scholars by and large didn't go to see it and worked instead from a text — do you see how he's engaging the history of art, even as he begins this religious painting? The point I'm going to make is: this is not sentimental Andy being religious near the end of his life, but rather he's engaging the whole history of Western art and how we've looked at this masterpiece. Have we ever looked at it? This is probably the text that you've had when you've looked at some of the reproductions. But it brings it down to our level, and then he puts these things on it. Now, the 59 cents. In the time in which he did it, that was the sale price. If you could get something for 59 cents, it doesn't come cheaper than that. So there it is: cheap commercialism. He was fascinated by it and collected cheap, vulgar reproductions of *The Last Supper*. He would go into these stores in Times Square and buy them. He was always fascinated by the popular image of an image. So, 59 cents. And then Dove soap: What's more American than Dove soap — put in front of Christ? And GE? GE makes our refrigerators, our air conditioners, and our light bulbs. Sacrilegious? No, not at all. Because what he's saying is, as we come to the religious experience of the divine, these are the filters. This is what he sees between us and our visioning of the spiritual, and it's crass, it's commercial, and he's part of it and so are we. I want to point something out. He was fascinated with consumerism 20 years before it was fashionable to write about it. Today, of course, everyone writes about the consumer culture. No one was writing about it when he did these paintings. He was ahead of his time. But he doesn't write about it, he shows it. The 59 cents. This is what stands between me and Christ. Dove. But each of these images has two sides, because the meal cleanses us from our sins through the Eucharist, and there's no better cleansing product than Dove. I think he's serious — the ambiguities, you see, the ambiguities.

Then we come to GE. Well, GE, Christ the light of the world: GE light bulbs. Isn't that a little bit simplistic? There are those who see the swirling lines as the image of creation. GE's motto was "We bring good things to light." And there are those who see here the Father reissue the world, and "Let there be light" is paired with "We bring good things to light." This is what mediates between Christ and us: a commercial culture, a culture of destruction that will eventually consume us.

I would suggest that when you have the time to look at his art, there's an enormous complexity that comes out of a deeply lived religious experience. Now, one or two things have to be said, because issues have been raised. "Oh well, he ran out of iconic images, so he turned himself to the Christ image." I think if you look at his life, the answer to that objection is no, no, no, no. It's more than that. I have statistics here, I'm going to read them. In the last two years of his life: 70 paintings of Christ, with 448 more images in the various series, for a total of 518 images of Jesus Christ in the last two years of his life. I would not say that's the work of somebody who's just looking for a new source of images. For those who like to dismiss him as a hypocrite — "There's the Andy Warhol of Studio 54, and then there's this Andy Warhol — well, hypocrisy is a dangerous thing to charge, first of all. And second of all, he had nothing to gain from it. Hypocrisy only serves if you're going to get something from it. He hid his religious life from most people. The whole point was that they didn't know about it. Only one or two friends, and they didn't take it very seriously. If he had revealed his religious dimension, they would have thought he was nuts. They wouldn't have stopped courting him, but they would have thought, "Ewww." There was nothing to be gained. Rather, Warhol stands as a prime example of the human condition: a man of faith, struggling to bring the different dimensions of his life together. The different components of his life had not yet been integrated, for he died quite young, at 58. We don't know where that journey would have gone.

I recommend Jane Daggett Dillenberger's book, *The Religious Art of Andy Warhol*, the only serious book that's been written about this.

Well, this brings us to Monsignor Luigi Giussani, for whom this is the religious sense. He saw it lurking in every work of art. This longing for something more, so obvious in the work of Warhol and others, whom at first we might dismiss as worldly and antithetical to the divine. An innate restlessness for totality and the infinite. I just want to point out that there are many other artists of the late 20th century for whom the religious sense explodes. Mark Rothko, with his paintings — paintings he saw as a search for the divine. George Tooker: people may not know George Tooker, but they know his paintings of frightening alienation in modern society. He was steeped in the loneliness and isolation of people living together in urban life. But then George Tooker, a lapsed Catholic, rediscovered his faith and created some of the most beautiful triptychs and polyptychs you could imagine, about which next to nothing is written. Or Keith Haring. Keith Haring the graffiti artist who died at age 31. Because of his early death, he has certainly becoming immortal. But no one writes about the religious dimension of his art. It is ignored totally. The image of the serpent and the cross, the image of the baby radiating light, and most importantly, his project for the Franciscan friars in the city of Pisa, where he worked to create this mural and shared meals with them and defined it as one of the most important communal experiences of his life. You will find nothing in the press, and yet it is the religious sense. How ironic that as our culture became less and less attuned to the divine in the 20th century, in art the religious sense increased and increased. Warhol was just one example.

Here's Andy in Milan, January 1987, one month before he died. He's with the Dominicans at his exhibition. In that particular exhibit, 12 gigantic paintings of *The Last Supper* are across the street from the original. He would go into a New York hospital a month later and die from a gall bladder operation. Andy Warhol is just one example of what Fr. Giussani spoke of when addressing the religious sense: those people — artists and others — who know that, in the end, only something infinite will suffice.

Thank you.

Something is Happening Here

*A presentation on Bob Dylan, the man and his music. With **Robert George**, McCormick Professor of Jurisprudence, Princeton University; **Richard F. Thomas**, George Martin Lane Professor of the Classics, Harvard University; and moderated by **Annemarie Bacich**, Educator and Curator of the Encounter exhibit*

Introduction

After nearly 60 years of composing songs, recording albums, and touring in concert, Bob Dylan remains as enigmatically appealing as when he first burst on the scene in the early 1960s. Arguably the most influential singer-songwriter in the history of rock and roll, Bob Dylan marked a point of no return for rock and roll, both musically and lyrically. Winner of the 2016 Nobel Prize in Literature, Dylan writes songs that are at once personal and universal, weaving tales simultaneously indecipherable and revelatory, turning a spotlight on the mystery of the human soul through glimpses of his own. This exhibit takes a look at Bob Dylan, the man and his music, recognizing along with Mister Jones that something is happening here worth paying attention to.

❖　❖　❖　❖　❖

Annemarie Bacich: Good afternoon and welcome to this conversation about the mesmeric Bob Dylan. My name is Annemarie Bacich, and I am the curator of the Bob Dylan exhibit t on the fifth floor here at the Encounter. I'm also high school teacher and have been an educator for about 20 years. This conversation today is meant as a compliment to the exhibit in which we're exploring the "something" that draws people to the work and art of Bob Dylan, and to the man Bob Dylan. We've invited two

Sunday, February 17, 2019

professors. They are both wise and accomplished in their own fields, and one I would say is an official Dylanologist. They have deep appreciation for Bob Dylan, the man and his music.

First, we have Richard Thomas, who is the George Martin Lane Professor of the Classics at Harvard University. He was educated at the University of Auckland and the University of Michigan. His teaching and research interests are focused on Hellenistic Greek and Roman literature — and the works of Bob Dylan. [*audience laughter and applause*] It's true! For the past 12 years, he's taught in the Classics Department one of the most popular seminars on Bob Dylan and his music. His publications include more than 100 articles and reviews and several books, the last one being 2017's *Why Dylan Matters*, which is actually on sale here; there will be a book signing right after this.

And then we have Professor Robert George. He is a McCormick Professor of Jurisprudence and Director of the James Madison Program in American Ideals and Institutions at Princeton University. He is the Chairman of the United States Commission on International Religious Freedom, and previously served on the President's Council on Bioethics and as a presidential appointee to the United States Commission on Civil Rights. A graduate of Swarthmore College and Harvard Law School, Professor George also earned a Master's in Theology from Harvard and a Doctorate in Philosophy of Law from Oxford University. The author of several books and innumerable articles, he holds honorary doctorates in law, literature, science, and ethics, and you can learn more about both of them in your program.

Arguably, Bob Dylan is the most influential singer-songwriter in rock and roll history, which isn't a long history. He marked a turning point for rock and roll, both musically and lyrically, and is the winner of the 2016 Nobel Prize in Literature. Dylan writes songs that are at once personal and universal, weaving tales simultaneously indecipherable and revelatory, turning a spotlight on the mystery of the human soul through glimpses of his own. Dylan taps into something and manages to express it, not only through his lyrics and music, but through the personas he embodies in his performances, and he is still performing today at 77 or 78 years of age.

Music critic Tom Moon wrote of Dylan's latest album — which came out during the planning of this exhibit — "He conjures the corkscrew to the heart then finds ways to turn it further [...] He's translating the messy and mysterious into music with universal resonance."

That is true for much of his work. Something is happening here in the work of Bob Dylan, and we hope to shed some light on it and go a little deeper into it this afternoon. I'd like to start with a question for you, Richard, and actually for Robert as well. Every die-hard Dylan fan, including myself, remembers what first drew them to his music. Perhaps it was a particular album. I remember the song and the moment that I knew I needed to explore more. Can you share with us how you first came to know and be interested in Bob Dylan, in his music?

Richard Thomas: I first became interested through *Blowing in the Wind*, but not sung by Bob Dylan. I'm nine years younger than Dylan, so that makes me 77 minus nine, and so we sang the Peter, Paul, and Mary version at a school choir when I was 13 or 14. The most memorable moment was a couple of years later, I guess, in '66, with *Sad-eyed Lady of the Lowlands*. A very good friend of my older brother had a girlfriend who dumped him, and he was very obsessed with that song. I heard it a lot and enjoyed it, all 11-plus minutes of it. It was a gradual process, but those are the two earliest moments I remember.

Robert George: Well, first I want to say just how delighted I am to be here, and how grateful I am for the invitation. Not only to be on this panel to discuss something I'm really interested in — Dylan's music — but also to be at this meeting. This is the first time for me at the New York Encounter. I've been to the wonderful Meeting in Rimini, but frankly, I didn't know about the New York Encounter. I'm really pleased to know about it and delighted to be here. It's such an honor to be on the panel with a genuine Dylan expert. I just like the music; Richard knows what he's talking about, so I'm hoping this will mostly be a conversation with Richard. But I can tell you a little bit about my first falling in love with Dylan's music. I'm a little younger, not a lot, but a little bit younger than Richard, so I don't quite remember firsthand *Blowing in the Wind* or *Times They Are a-Changin'*, much less the earlier folk stuff from the Newport

Festival. I have since gone back and looked at YouTube and so forth, but I got interested in Dylan in the late 1960s when he put out *Nashville Skyline Rag*. By that time — I was born and brought up in West Virginia — I was interested in country music. I was playing guitar and banjo, and Dylan, who was from a school of music, rock and roll, I had very little interest in, had suddenly put out a really interesting country album that even had Johnny Cash on it. So, wow! I got really fascinated with that, and that got me interested in Dylan himself. Then I went back and discovered the wonderful stuff from earlier in the 1960s and even the late 1950s, which I've come to love and have performed often myself. So it was really the country iteration of Dylan that brought me through the door.

Thomas: I should just add that when I got my first girlfriend, *Lay Lady Lay* was out. [*audience laughter*] My mother didn't like that.

Bacich: As Joan Baez said, when Dylan touches somebody in a particular way, he really goes deep. What I found interesting in doing this work, and in talking with other Dylan aficionados, is that his music draws you in if you're serious with him. I was wondering if you could speak to what it is about Dylan and his work that draws so many people in and then doesn't disappoint.

Thomas: Right, well it happens with the political songs and civil rights songs and anti-war songs that he happens to be a genius. The one mark of a genius is to be able to do what we can't do, but to create something that is meaningful to us as human beings. So as Todd Gitlin said — Dylan, of course, was trying to lose his protest singer label — "Dylan wrote our songs for us whether he liked it or not, he produced our songs for us." And I think that's true not just through his songwriting, but also through his performance, through the look of him, through the voice. He touches our souls in any number of ways, because he can write the songs that we can't write, songs that are utterly meaningful in every complex way it means to be a human being.

His songs since 1997 are the songs not of a young man. He's not up there like Mick, with leather pants on, pretending, singing songs of a 19- or 20-year-old. He's singing songs that are still about love, lovesickness, and so on, the condition is still there, the unavoidable condition, the attempt to escape — but now one is drawn back in through memory, through the pain of an experience that mattered but is no longer there and only your mind. He's an older, wiser Dylan. I stopped listening in '79, because I was not a person of faith and felt betrayed. I came back to him later, with faith. But if you start listening to him, start in '97 and just listen to the music that he's produced. It's absolutely astonishing. I think *Tempest* is as good an album as *Blonde on Blonde*, the one album I brought with me from New Zealand.

George: Well he's certainly capable of provoking or eliciting powerful reactions from people. The best evidence for that is Joan Baez's *Diamonds and Rust*. Toxic masculinity has never been as powerfully indicted as it was by Baez in that song, which of course is about Dylan's mistreatment of her. It's really a great song. Joan Baez is not a great songwriter; she's a wonderful singer, but he elicited from her — even if in an unfortunate manner — that really powerful song. The other thing that draws people in is the "Americanness" of Bob Dylan. He couldn't be anything else. He couldn't be French, or Chinese, or Saudi, or Brazilian. He's distinctively American. There's a kind of ruthlessness, that search for roots, a desire to be rooted but not *too* rooted, a desire to be able to create and recreate yourself but not be entirely alien, not be entirely detached. Dylan has created and recreated himself, but I think it's more than simply creating and recreating personae. I think it's actually real. I think he has experienced transformations. Now, there are also the masks, we all know about the masks, that's for sure. But I think there are also these transformations. I think in the American psyche, there's a tension and a drama about whether we create ourselves, or discover our true selves, so when we go on the quest, is the quest to discover the real me? Or is it a quest of self-creation, to decide just for ourselves, for our own reasons or for no reasons at all, that we want to be this or that or the other thing? In my judgment, for what it's worth, I think Dylan comes out consistently on the side of self-discovery more than self-creation. There's something very American about that. And it's also important that Dylan is from the periphery and away from the heartland. How can he be the periphery? He's a major force in American culture, and certainly in American *elite* culture, but he's not *from* the elite culture. He's growing up in the '40s, I guess, the '50s. He is starting to do music in the '50s. This is a White Anglo-Saxon Protestant America, and he's a Jewish kid. Not from New York. Not from L.A. He's not Ivy League. He's this amazing person from the hinterlands, but very American in that.

Bacich: Thank you. In fact, that is a perfect segue: his quintessential Americanness. When you watch videos of him during the height of his fame in the mid-'60s, and in Europe people would ask him about his songs and he'd say, "Are you American?" because they didn't understand. He'd say, "This is American music — are you American?" H had a clear perception of that. I'm tempted to talk about that Joan Baez song, which I would have never characterized in the way you did, as toxic masculinity, but I won't; I digress. She still says that he's the most brilliant, crazy person she's ever known, so she still has a great affection for Bob Dylan.

George: If I can just follow up on that. In *Diamonds and Rust*, for those of you who know it is, he's calling from the phone booth in the Midwest, and I think he's actually reading her the lyrics of *Lily, Rosemary and the Jack of Hearts*. He hasn't been in touch; they haven't been in touch in a long time.

Bacich: In years.

George: He calls her from the phone booth somewhere in the Midwest, he reads her the lyrics to this new song he has written, he's obviously very pleased with himself about it. But one of the things that Baez reports in the song is: My poetry is lousy, you said. So one of the ways that he offended or hurt her was by telling her, perhaps truthfully, that her poetry is lousy, but actually, her poetry in *Diamonds and Rust* is pretty good.

Bacich: Yes. Absolutely.

Thomas: Also, you who are so good with words, I think she captures Dylan the songwriter. Of course, I think it's in *Rolling Thunder* that he suggested she play the song, and she said she played the Dylan card. She said, "Well, that wasn't to you, that was about someone else." [*audience laughter*]

Bacich: Dylan says all of his work is autobiographical. I mean, at the same time, especially in his early stuff and things through *Blood on the Tracks*, there's a sort of a veiled poetic "I" in there, and this brings me to a question.

We just spoke about his quintessential Americanness, but it's also clear that he has an incredible international appeal. He won the Nobel Prize in Literature, which was pretty controversial in 2016. I wanted to ask you, in particular, Richard, because many people were surprised by the choice. In fact, some people in the establishment were disgruntled at this singer-songwriter who had sort of stolen the poet's laurels when he was a kid, now is getting the prize in 2016. I'd like you to speak as a professor of literature and classics: Why do you think it's such a controversial choice, and why do you think it makes sense in the context of world literature, in classical literature, that he won the prize?

Thomas: Americanness is appreciated in Japan, for example, where he's very popular with people who don't know a word of English. The look, the voice, the music, the sound, the lyrics. As for the Nobel, I was one of the people that had been pushing for it for years. A friend of mine, Robert Ball, has written about nominating Bob for the Nobel for years, and I think the committee eventually heard and saw what was involved with Dylan. For me, Dylan is up there Virgil and Homer and Ovid, a poet he's been channeling since 2001. *Love and Theft* started with Virgil. Why do I teach him? I think he's a classic, in the same way that they are classics. I don't know if they'll be around in 200 years, the way this world and this country are headed — I'm an American citizen, by the way, so I can say that — but if anybody's song is listened to, and if songs still exist and songs exist before literature, Bob Dylan will still be around in the same way that those poets are around, and he'll be around because his songs touch what it means to be a human being. Human nature doesn't change, and so experience doesn't change. Therefore, the expression, the artistic and creative capturing of what it means to be human, will remain constant. 1

Song and poetry come together. A member of the Swedish Academy, Sara Danius, said, "Sappho was sung in antiquity. We've lost the music but we can still read it as poetry." Dylan actually contradicted that in his June 2017 Nobel lecture, when he starts talking about song at the end. He has a wonderful story from the *Odyssey*. Odysseus meets the shade of Achilles in the underworld, and Achilles says, "I just died, that's all. It wasn't about fame." Then Dylan makes the transition to talking about songs. "My songs are in the land of the living," he says. He constinues: "My songs have to be sung; they can't be read." So in his speech accepting the Nobel Prize for Literature, he contradicted the head of the Academy that awarded it to him. It's amusing in a way, but that's the integrity of Bob Dylan the artist. He was happy to get the Nobel, but he was not going to allow his art to be redefined into something it isn't, namely, words without music. That is just the courage, the honesty of Dylan, who knows where he's going. He knew three or four years before the rest of us, at d various stages in his career, so he deserves it.

George: Well, I don't know nearly as much as Richard does, so I was caught by surprise. I didn't know anyone was pushing for this. I was just one of those people who was stunned that he got the Nobel Prize. I just didn't think the Nobel Prize went to people like Bob Dylan, because there are no people like Bob Dylan. But what did not surprise me a bit, in fact, was that he didn't show up to get it. That was completely unsurprising for me. Richard pointed out at lunch that Dylan had to give the lecture in order to collect the $990,000, so it's not surprising that he gave the lecture [*audience laughter*] — but I wasn't surprised that he didn't show up for it.

Two themes run through a lot of the music in the different periods: the Christian period, the country period, the rock and roll period, the phone period. Two themes are: freedom and belonging. And those two are also often in tension. When we belong, we need to conform, we need to be with the group. There are norms, there are rules. And then we long for freedom. But freedom can also be self-alienating. We need a sense of belonging, being part of something again, being rooted. A lot of people thought of Dylan early on — and continue to think of him — as a protest singer. He always denies that, and indeed even his liberation songs are not easily classified as protest songs. But am I right that these themes run through his music?

Thomas: Sure. He wrote the best civil rights song and the best anti-war song ever written, and so it's the songs that he produced through his genius that allow us to get close to those feelings about freedom, about belonging. Did Bob Dylan oppose the Vietnam War? I imagine he probably did. He wasn't on tour from '66 to '74, when it was really heating up. He wasn't in Chicago in '68 or Paris in '68, so I just don't know. He's also said, "Aren't all of my songs protest songs?" And in a sense, they are: protests about the unfair things that happen in life, including unjust wars. And then he's done things like singing *Masters of War* as we were about to bomb Iraq — aided by Australia and New Zealand — leading up to that event in early 2003. The minute we went in, he stopped singing it and it disappeared from the set list, because I think he didn't want to be labeled by singing it as the bombs were falling.

I've been to the Tulsa archive four times, and you see in the archive just how much care he's putting into his songs. There are songs there that have a bridge that's finished, and have the first line that's finished, but the structure of the song, and the meaning of the song, and the meanings of the song, are not yet there. They come gradually through the hard work that Dylan has as an artist. He did *Blowing in the Wind* in 10 minutes. Look at the structure of that song, that incredibly artful song. Dylan is a very unreliable narrator, as we all know, and so all we have are the songs. Dylan has made sure that all we have are the songs, and performances of them by Dylan. He's just — there's not been anyone like him in the last 50 years.

Bacich: We've spoken here about the human experience and how Bob Dylan is able to really tap into that through his art. I'd like to approach the religious question. I mean, from very early on, in Dylan the human person is a religious being, someone who seeks to understand what this life is about. What I discovered in researching Dylan is his perception of himself as being on a journey, and his perception of himself as having been given a gift. He talks about this in an interview when he was 23 years old. Although Dylan gives us only his music, he also endorses books like *The Essential Interviews*, in which there are quite a few interviews where he explicitly talks about his Christianity, his conversion, and especially his fascination with the person of Christ. He has three albums that are confessional albums, the three Gospel albums. Some critics talk about that as having been a phase, but I'd like both of you to speak about his religiosity, in particular the experience of his conversion, and how that's continued or changed since the late '70s.

George: Well, one of the most insightful things I've ever heard anybody say about Donald Trump, is that Trump's critics made the mistake of taking him literally but not seriously. To understand him, you have to take him seriously but not literally. There's a sense in which that's true of Bob Dylan as well. He tells a lot of — for want of a better word — fibs, especially about himself, his own history, his own background, and what's going on inside his head. But I'm using the word fib rather than lie, and maybe even fib is too strong a word, because I have a sense that to understand him, especially on the religious question, you can't take him literally but you have to take him seriously, because he's serious about it. Richard can confirm whether this is true. Dylan says he attended a Billy Graham rally and he found it absolutely exhilarating, because Billy Graham was not only a mesmerizing preacher but was saving souls. And Dylan makes clear — at least to the extent that you can take him literally — that he didn't mean anything sarcastic by saving souls; he didn't mean saving souls in some figurative sense; he meant *literally* saving people's souls. What he's talking about here, about attending that rally and having that experience, in forming that judgment, was before his formal conversion and before the period of the three Gospel albums. My sense is that he was serious about religion, and not just the abstract meaning-of-life stuff. I mean, dogmatic faith: is Jesus Christ the Son of God? Did He die on a cross for the redemption of mankind and the forgiveness of sins? He's dealing with those questions and wrestling with those questions, and having what can only be described as a religious experience at a Billy Graham rally. If it actually happened, of course, and I'd like Richard to tell us whether it did. But even if it didn't, if it's one of the fibs that he tells, it's got to be taken seriously even if you can't take it literally. He's wrestling with questions of faith — concrete, specific, Who-is-Jesus-Christ-type questions of faith. So, was he at the Billy Graham rally?

Thomas: Yeah, yeah. But he was also bar mitzvah'd at the Androy Hotel in Hibbing, Minnesota. Go to Hibbing if you haven't been there. Go to Duluth also, both places. The fight for the soul of Bob Dylan: Is he Jewish? Is he Christian? He's Jewish. He's never not been. I have a friend who's a rabbi in Minnesota, he knows where Dylan went for some years, but yes, he had a conversion experience. He draws from the Hebrew Bible and the New Testament. In *Shelter from the Storm*, of course, he is Christ. "In a little hilltop village they gambled for my clothes." That may seem shocking, but the "I" there is that figure, and audacity of Dylan is that he's willing to do that. That might seem like irreverence. I don't think it is. I think it's part of just the profound lyric-making of Dylan. Take the song *Cold Irons Bound*: "I went to church on Sunday and she passed by." And then *Not Dark Yet*: "I was born here and I'll die here, against my will." Those are two songs on the same album, but draw from the faith liturgies of both religions. Unlike Leonard Cohen, I don't think he's dabbled much in Eastern literature, but I assume he's a man of faith. I don't think he could write the songs that he has written otherwise. People tried to pin him down: "Oh look, he went to Jerusalem, he must have come back," which reflected a natural desire to get Dylan back to his Jewishness. But *Slow Train Coming* is an undeniably Christian song. Pick a song like *Every Grain of Sand*. *Every Grain of Sand* doesn't mention Jesus, but God cares about every grain of sand. Anybody of any religion can have a faith experience by listening to the poetry of that song. The captain on the Titanic in *Tempest*: "He read the Book of Revelation and he filled his cup with tears." Fantastic. He's talking around the issue a bit, but I think he knows what his faith is. It's complex and it embraces a great deal, including the Christianity he learned about by attending Sunday school in those months.

George: Evidently in his performances, even his recent performances, he still does some of the Gospel numbers. After a concert someone said to him, "You know, you sang that like a true believer." And he responded, "I *am* a true believer." But going way back, when someone in the crowd hollered "Judas" at him — was that when he went electric?

Thomas: Well, yeah. That was in England, where he was doing acoustic the first half and electric the second half. And the fans in England — you can see it in Scorsese's documentary — the fans from '65 just were blown away, because the Dylan who had just again reached them at their core had disappointed them. Dylan knew he was born to play with a band, and with electric as well as acoustic instruments. He knew that and he made the transition, and eventually people caught up with him. There's discussion about how much booing there was. Seeger claims he didn't try to cut the cables, it's just that the sound was terrible. If you were going to hear an acoustic *Mister Tambourine Man* and instead you hear Mike Bloomfield's electric guitar howling out into the night — yeah, something had happened.

George: Someone hollered out, "Judas!" Later, when he was asked why it had upset him so much, he responded: "Beecause he accused me of being the person who betrayed our Savior."

Bacich: That was in 2012.

Thomas: That was that tongue in cheek: "Our Savior."

George: Take him seriously but not literally.

Thomas: The Judas shout comes out of the dark, and Dylan, who's probably pretty drugged-up at this point — the motorcycle accident happened a bit later — said, "I don't believe you! You're a liar!" And then he turns to Robbie Robertson and says, "Play fucking loud." He comes around and gestures with the guitar on the opening note of *Like a Rolling Stone*. This is Dylan saying, "This is what I give you back for calling me that." So in his performance, he gave an answer.

Bacich: To both of you: What is your favorite Dylan song and why?

Thomas: It depends. It was one thing two hours ago, it's another thing now. It's whatever I'm listening to on my iPod. I need an iPod because I have lots of songs. *Visions of Johanna* is probably the poetic song that most touches me. *Every Grain of Sand. Not Dark Yet.* I came down for one of the Beacon shows in December. They have a beautiful version of *Scarlet Town*, completely unlike the studio version, but for that moment and for days afterwards, that was my favorite Dylan song. It's partly recalling him in performance. Oh, and *More Blood, More Tracks* — if you haven't gotten that, get it.

Bacich: It's wonderful.

George: I was rolling around in my mind, trying to think of what my favorite Dylan song is, and it is very hard. I'm not going to be able to come up with an answer, I'm afraid. There are at least three categories of

Dylan songs for me, and I'll tell you what my favorite is in each. One is the common human experience thing, and a lot of those have to do with the boy-girl thing: falling in love, having fights, falling out of love, a relationship breaks apart, whatever. For me, you just can't beat *Don't Think Twice It's All Right*. I love that song. It's pretty straightforward, it's not difficult to understand what the meaning is, or what's going on in the song. The next category is the ballad-type song, and he's got so many wonderful ones. The one that just draws me in is *Lily, Rosemary and the Jack of Hearts*. I think that's an extraordinary piece of music. The third category is: "I'm not sure the song has any meaning." I can't give up the quest to figure it out, despite my colleague, the wonderful Dylanologist, telling me, "Robbie, it doesn't mean anything. You can give it up." And in that category, my absolute favorite is *She Belongs to Me*. That's an obscure one.

Thomas: *Love Minus Zero/No Limit.*

George: But there are several good covers of it as well. "She belongs to me..."

Thomas and Bacich: "She's got everything she needs, she's an artist, she don't look back..."

George: "...take the dark out of the nighttime and paint the daytime black." But will somebody tell me what it means to say, "She wears an Egyptian ring that sparkles before she speaks"? I've been working on that for about 40 years. [*audience laughter*]

Thomas: But don't you have an image of her?

George: I do, I absolutely do!

Bacich: Well, thank you; this has been wonderful, and we could go on for hours, but we'll stop now.

A New Beginning. Life in the Aftermath of a Massacre

*Witnesses on the Sandy Hook massacre. With **Fr. Peter Cameron, OP**, Director of Formation of Hard As Nails Ministries; **Dawn Ford**, Educator, survivor of the Sandy Hook massacre; and **Jenny Hubbard**, mother of Catherine Violet, murdered in the Sandy Hook massacre*

Introduction

Very often, in front of a terrible tragedy, our instinct is to look away or to come up with quick solutions so that the unspeakable horror will never happen again. However, deep down we know that such problems are not easily solvable because evil cannot be completely eradicated, neither in ourselves, nor in the other. Therefore, in front of evil, a more urgent and real question is: How can we live with what already happened? How can you begin again? Where do you start from? There are some people who cannot evade this question, nor take refuge in the endless debates about what to do. They are those who have been directly hit by the loss of a loved one, by the direct experience of senseless violence. Not only do we need to look at them in order to learn how it is possible to go on living in the face of tragedy but, paradoxically, they may also be the ones who can think most clearly about what can be done, for the simple reason that the experience of a great suffering makes them painfully aware of reality in all its complexity and depth.

For these reasons we are profoundly grateful to Dawn Ford, Jenny Hubbard, and Fr. Peter Cameron who have accepted to share with us their experience of sorrow, struggle, hope, and life.

Sunday, February 17, 2019

❖ ❖ ❖ ❖ ❖

Fr. Peter Cameron: Welcome and thank you for coming. My name is Fr. Peter John Cameron. We have to begin by remembering something that is terrible beyond words. On Friday, December 14th, 2012, a deranged young man from Newtown, Connecticut, murdered his sleeping mother. He then loaded his car with several guns and hundreds of rounds of ammunition and drove five miles to Sandy Hook Elementary School. He blasted a hole through the security glass near the school's locked front door and set upon a bloody rampage. Within five minutes he had murdered 20 first-graders, six and seven years old. He also murdered six educators. The gunman then shot himself to death.

For some reason, the central meeting point after this atrocity was Saint Rose of Lima Catholic Church in nearby Newtown. Eight of the ensuing funerals for the victims were held at Saint Rose of Lima. From the years 2009 to 2014, I served as the weekend associate priest there. My job was to help celebrate the Sunday Masses at the parish. On the morning of December 14th, 2012, a friend from Newtown called my cellphone to tell me that a shooting had taken place at the nearby Sandy Hook Elementary School. I immediately drove from Yonkers, New York, where I was living at the time, to Saint Rose of Lima. I was present at the impromptu Mass held in the church that evening, which about 2,000 people attended, including the governor of Connecticut. And now, an unbelievable six years have gone by.

In the summer of 2012, I was on a trip to Poland to give a workshop, and I asked my host while I was there if it might be possible for me to visit the Auschwitz concentration camp. He arranged a visit and we went. It was a harrowing experience; the visit concluded with a tour of the second concentration camp that is very close by, Birkenau. That camp contains what was originally called The International Monument to the Victims of Fascism. Unveiled in 1967, it bears a plaque that, in a number of different languages, declares forever: "Let this place be a cry of despair and a warning to humanity, where the Nazis murdered about 1 1/2 million men, women, and children." I was stunned by this. A warning to humanity, yes — but isn't there something more than a cry of despair? If we stop there, if we stop at that, then life itself becomes impossible. We need a different kind of cry. We always need the possibility of a new beginning. We need something to start from. Some of you will recall the alarm that gripped this country between the years 1978 and 1995, when the terrorist, known as the Unabomber, carried out a nationwide bombing spree by way of the United States postal system, which targeted academics and technology experts. He killed three people and injured 23 others, including Yale University professor David Gelernter. Upon recuperating from a nearly fatal mail bombing, he wrote this: "Although I was hurt permanently and will never get back a normal right hand or right eye, although my chest will always look like a gouged-out construction site, here is the main thing: I recovered. In some ways, I am better than before. If you insert into this weird slot machine of modern life one evil act, a thousand acts of kindness tumble out."

Flashing back to 2010, as I stood there in the Nazi concentration camp, reading the plaque on the Birkenau Memorial and feeling pretty depressed, I looked up and saw something that I will never forget. It was a Catholic priest who had with him a group of young people. They were all gathered around him and the priest was getting ready to do something. He was preparing to celebrate Mass right there in the concentration camp, in that place of unspeakable hatred and barbarity. And I thought, yes, that is the better cry. A cry for something that perceives a promise even within the most challenging circumstances of life.

Today we are blessed and honored to have with us two exceptional women who are here to help us cry out for that something. We are honored to have with us Jennifer Hubbard. Jennifer's youngest child, Catherine Violet, was a victim of the Sandy Hook Elementary School shooting. Jennifer has established the Catherine Violet Hubbard Foundation in her daughter's memory. The foundation is currently building the Catherine Violet Hubbard Animal Sanctuary in Newtown. Jennifer currently serves as chair and president of the sanctuary. She was also a monthly contributor to *Magnificat* and the recipient of the 2014 and 2015 Catholic Press Awards, and I can attest to the fact that Jenny Hubbard is one of *Magnificat*'s best-loved writers. One month after the Sandy Hook school shooting, Saint Rose of Lima church presented a series of talks for the parents of the children and the religious education program, as the children were preparing to return to school for the first time since the shooting. As you can imagine, it was a tremendously anxiety-ridden time. The point of the program was to help the children and the parents make the transition as easy as possible. The Director of Religious Education for the parish, Pam, was very close to the eight mothers from the parish who had lost children in the massacre. Those eight mothers became very close after December 14th, and Pam mentioned to Jenny what the parish was planning to do to help the parents. Well, when Jennifer Hubbard learned that the parish was going to hold this gathering, she did something that no one ever expected. She decided on her own that she wanted to come in person and speak to the assembled parents face to face, and that is what she did. I was asked to moderate that session, and in preparation for it I called Jenny on the phone. During our conversation, I asked her how it was ever possible for her to do something that most of the world would consider completely impossible to do. And Jenny responded by saying this: there is a presence that is so much better than us, and we have to acknowledge it. When the day arrived, as she stood in the pulpit of Saint Rose of Lima and addressed a church full of parents, what she said, and the way that she said it, was utterly amazing. It was, as I told her afterwards, like listening to Saint Catherine of Siena speak. You will see that for yourselves shortly. And when the other mothers heard that Jenny was going to go speak to the parents, some of them also volunteered to go and speak at the parish sessions.

Today we are also deeply honored to have with us Dawn Ford. Dawn Ford was born and raised in Danbury, Connecticut. She received a Bachelor of Science degree in Biology from the State University of New York at Brockport. Early in her career, she worked in the fields of chemistry and environmental science. After the birth of her three children, she pursued a Master's degree in teaching from Sacred Heart University. She taught second grade for ten years at Sandy Hook Elementary School in Newtown, and for the past five years Dawn has been teaching sixth grade math and science at Reed Intermediate School, also in Newtown. Dawn has been married for 33 years to Steve, and Steve is here. She and her husband have called Newtown their home for the past 28 years, and we are also very pleased that Dawn's mother, Joyce, is here and her sister Kelly. We welcome you, we're so happy you are with us.

If you look at the Wikipedia page about the Sandy Hook school shooting, you will read this remark: "Some of those present in the school heard the initial gunshots on the school intercom system, which was being used for morning announcements." You need to know that that comment simply isn't true. Those are not the facts, and that is not how it happened. It has nothing to do with the reality of that day, and we who feel so urgently the need to discover our identity and somehow start again really need those facts, because of the breathtaking way they make us feel looked at, listened to, understood, and valued. To say that the true story that Dawn is about to tell you is phenomenal and flabbergasting doesn't come close to the truth of it — but it is true. We have to begin again by remembering something awesome beyond words, and we are so grateful that Dawn is here to help us do that. Please welcome now Dawn Ford.

Dawn Ford: Thank you, Fr. Peter. My audience is usually kids, second-graders, and then sixth-graders, so I'm a little nervous. I do have notes to read from. It is from my heart, but I don't want to lose track, so I hope you'll forgive me that I have my notes.

On the morning of December 14th, 2012, I had a meeting first thing, which was to begin in the conference room of our school. I walked into that meeting at 9:33 after briefing my sub of the morning math plans. There were eight others in the room, including Dawn Hochsprung, our principle; Mary Sherlach, our school psychologist; Natalie Green, our lead teacher; a parent whose child we were meeting about; and various other support staff. No sooner had Mary opened up the meeting than we heard from the hallway three loud pops — POP POP POP — but much louder. I didn't know what it was; it sounded to me like chairs falling, like maybe the custodians were setting up something in the cafeteria. Many of us stood from our seats, and I remembered Dawn and I locked eyes, she was saying, "What was that?" as she was sweeping out of the room, followed by Natalie and Mary. As soon as they left our conference room, the hallway erupted in gunfire. We scattered to the four corners of the room, still not comprehending what exactly was going on. To me, I had nothing in my experience to tell me that that was what was happening. I thought it was fireworks, which also doesn't make sense, that fireworks would be going on outside. But, there would be a barrage of gunfire, followed by momentary silence, followed by more gunfire. During one of the momentary silences, Natalie Ham, and not Green — Green was her maiden name — Natalie silently slipped back into the room, hopping on one foot because she had been shot up one side of her body: her leg, her foot, and her hand. She whispered, "Dawn and Mary are down," and she laid herself down and pressed herself up against the front wall of our conference room, and she held our conference room door closed with her good hand. The gunfire erupted again. During the next silence someone whispered, "We have to call for help, does anybody have a phone?" And at that time, the only cell-phone in the room was in the parent's purse, and her purse was on the table that was in direct view of the window to our conference room. So, nobody dared to reach for it. There was a phone on the wall, and if I had stood, I could have picked up the phone and dialed, but then, I would have been in direct vision of the window. Not wanting to be that visible, I reached up and batted the phone off the hook and left the receiver dangling from the cord, and I reached up to punch the code that would get us an outside line so I could call 911. But no sooner had I started punching in the series of numbers, gunfire erupted again. I retreated back to my corner and forgot about that phone; I just left it dangling. Silence came again. It seemed to be longer this time. We dared to believe that whatever it was was over, but we still didn't dare emerge from the room. There was a different kind of silence in the hall, a different kind of activity — it was hushed movements, and we were hopeful that it was help. Someone said we need to pray and began reciting the Our Father. I crawled at this point, from my spot in the corner to Natalie, and I just slipped my knees under her head so she could rest her head. Although she was lying on the floor, she was just holding her head up, very tense, not resting, and I replaced my hand with hers on the door. So, although we thought it was maybe over, we still were protecting ourselves in our room. Another coworker came from the other corner of the room to Natalie's feet and just stroked her legs, and soothed her, encouraging her to breathe. It felt like an endless amount of time as we waited, but finally a police officer gingerly opened the door, and emergency personnel took Natalie to a waiting ambulance.

They didn't want us to leave; we were told to stay put. So I think at this time they didn't know if there was one or multiple perpetrators, and they didn't want to move people who didn't require medical attention. But at this point, we did feel that it was safe to move about the room, so I grabbed the parent's purse and handed it to her and we took turns making phone calls. I called my husband, Steve, who worked just down the street at his shop, and I reported to him that there were multiple gunshots fired inside of our school. And our adult son, who was 22 at the time, was in the school, working in the library. Ben has autism, and I was very afraid that he would be very vocal and draw attention to himself, but I later learned from the women who work with him in the library that when they heard the gunfire, they knew to go into lockdown, and they led him to a supply room in the back of the library. He went quietly, and quietly followed their directions. And once inside that closet he found a bag of stuffed animals, and he pulled each one out silently, and surrounded himself for comfort. Didn't say a word.

Once we were able to leave the conference room, we walked past Mary and Dawn, who were lying in the hallway, and even as they took Natalie to a waiting ambulance and Natalie said what she said, I still couldn't quite process what was happening. I didn't understand why nobody was helping Mary and Dawn. Why are they just lying there? But I didn't realize until later that there was nothing they could do. Exiting the building, we walked over the shattered glass that was the entry to our school. We were among the first people to walk out of the building and we were directed to go to the firehouse at the end of our driveway; that was our emergency evacuation location. But I couldn't leave. I didn't know where my second-grade class was, I didn't know where my son was, and I quickly met up with Steve in the parking lot, because he was on the scene before many of the first responders. He directed me to wait for my second grade class while he went to find Ben. So I headed back to the building but, of course, I wasn't let in, and so I paced the parking lot until my second grade class came out, led by our building sub, Kathleen, who I will forever be grateful to for how she took care of my class that day.

In the weeks that followed once the investigation was complete, the staff was called together for a debriefing by the police before they were to release the final report to the public. And among the details of the investigation was a statement that the single event that saved the most lives that day was the fact that the PA system had been opened and broadcast the shooting throughout the school. Our school was a big rectangle and we were in the front of the school; and people in the back of the school, if they hadn't heard that through the loudspeaker, they may have heard something was going on but they may not have known, and then potentially there could have been a lot more people in the hall. Kids bringing notes to the office, or even adults investigating, you know, sounds that they had heard. Although distressing to hear, it alerted them to go into lockdown, and everybody did exactly what they were supposed to do.

The lieutenant in charge of the investigation added that the remarkable part about this detail was that the PA system was activated by the phone in the conference room — which had been left dangling off the hook. But the phone in the conference room was not wired to do that. The only phone that was wired to broadcast throughout the school was in the front office, which was not attached to our conference room. Which is probably why Wikipedia says that, because that's the only phone that was wired. So, at this point, the staff members questioned, "What are you saying? Are you saying it was an act of God?" And the lieutenant shrugged his shoulders and said, "I have no explanation." Although I still can't comprehend the answer to the question, "Why does God allow this to happen?" I feel that although He didn't or couldn't control one man's act of free will, the answer to the question, "Where was God that day?" is that He was there. I believe He was there to lift all those souls straight to heaven and I believe He was there for the rest of us who survived.

In the aftermath there was a huge outpouring of support from around the country, and even around the world, to some extent, and I just want to focus on a few examples. In thinking of the theme of the Encounter, I thought about this one example. When we left our school abruptly on December 14th, we didn't know at first that we wouldn't be together again as a school until after the first of the year. We had no closure with our students. They left us scared and traumatized that day, with no plan for when we would come back. So, someone thought it would be a good idea if we were able to get together with our students before school reconvened. In a casual atmosphere, which was a great idea. Another second grade teacher arranged for some of our classes to get together in the meeting room of our public library, and when we got there I was amazed at what

I saw. The room was completely decorated for Christmas. There was a Christmas tree, there were crafts for the kids to do, gingerbread houses for them to make, and of course, there were books. There was a mountain of stuffed animals that they were immediately diving into and crawling under and through like a ball pit, and everybody got to take one home. The thing that was astonishing to me about that day was that the library staff member who put the celebration together was someone I had just known as an acquaintance. I'd known her for a long time just as an acquaintance, because she had been with the library for a long time, and this was a person I didn't know well, but I had had some encounters with her and had witnessed encounters. I had never had, nor witnessed, a positive interaction between her and another person, ever. I was actually kind of scared of her. I just looked at her in awe, and something in my heart changed toward her that day, because I did not have a very high opinion of her. But my opinion of her changed that day, and I thought maybe there's more to this person then I realized.

Another significant example was the school that we were given. Our neighboring town of Monroe actually gave us a school. They had a middle school that they weren't using; it was empty and they allowed us to occupy it for as long as we needed until our new school was built — which ended up being years. But this was significant because there was talk of us not going back to Sandy Hook. There was talk of us being scattered all over town in empty retail spaces, in empty office spaces, so this gift of a school gave us the opportunity to come back together as a school community and begin the healing process together. The most moving part of this was that, when we arrived at the school over our winter break to set up our classrooms, we found that people were already there. Other teachers from our Newtown school district; but not only them, people from the Monroe school district, their friends and their neighbors were there, making a school for our elementary school kids. Decorating bulletin boards with snow scenes, and gingerbread scenes, and Candyland scenes. As a teacher, I realize how precious that time is. Seems like a long break, but it's not a long break, what with two holidays and visiting family and trying to get a little rest. So, these people were here, giving their winter holiday time, their rest and rejuvenate time, and their family time, to build a school for us and our kids. I remember walking in and encountering these people who are cheerily doing this work, not grudgingly. They were joyfully doing this work and I was overwhelmed with gratitude.

Support came in many forms besides the physical school building. It came in the form of things, gifts that were sent to us — anything you can imagine: prayer shawls, meals, show tickets, jewelry; you just can't even imagine the things. And for the kids: toys, stuffed animals, school supplies, sporting events; and although I appreciated where the thought came from for sending these gifts and services, and that was from a place of helplessness and wanting to do something, for me the things offered little comfort. However, in addition to the things, there were also notes and cards sent by kids, students in schools around the country, and around the world, teachers and the general public. These were short, heartfelt notes, wishing thoughts of care and concern and healing. These thoughts and prayers, whether spoken or unspoken, written or unwritten, along with the direct support from my family and friends, filled me with a sense of calm and peace, even though my heart was broken. I did not feel alone. I felt overwhelmed with gratitude for both the support from my family and friends and from people who I didn't know and would never meet.

So… something to start from. In response to a horrific tragedy like the one we experienced, there is an overwhelming feeling that something must be done, some kind of action must be taken. I felt this almost immediately. Well, what am I supposed to do? Why am I still here? Besides the obvious, which was to continue to live my life, I had a family to take care of, I had students to teach, friends to enjoy. But these questions have been on my mind over the past six years. I've reflected on my experiences, not only being in that place on that day, but mostly what I experienced in the aftermath and how those experiences affected me. I was deeply moved by people's responses and I continue to be moved by the good in people. I'm going to borrow words now from authors who could articulate my feelings better than I can. One author, Brant Hansen, in his book *Blessed are the Misfits*, said something so simple yet so profoundly true. He was speaking in response to the manmade tragedies in life, like what happened to us at Sandy Hook; when people say — mostly the news media — "We don't need prayers, we need action," Hanson suggests that prayer *is* action and prayer changes hearts; when one heart is changed, there's a ripple effect that is far reaching. Another author, Matthew Kelly, in his book *The Biggest Lie in the History of Christianity*, says that when hearts change, people act in holy ways. And he advocates creating holy moments on a daily basis, and by holy moments he's simply referring to acts of kindness, both big and small. I realize what I experienced and continue to experience are holy moments.

I mentioned that our son Ben has autism. He's now almost 29 years old. He has four part-time jobs in our community, including his job at Sandy Hook school, which he still holds today. Although I moved on, he wanted to stay there. Ben's lucky in many ways. He has a group of friends that he's been with since elementary school; he has a busy social life. Between his job and his social activities, it gets him out in the community. He has weekly activities and monthly activities — dinners out, bowling, working out at the gym. He doesn't drive, and so he depends on people to get him to his activities; but he has all these activities because of his community. Ben likes his own company and he likes his alone time, and if given the chance, he would spend endless hours on video games and watching YouTube videos. Without his community involvement, he would very, very, easily slip into isolation, disconnected from people. Unfortunately, there are many people who are marginalized for a variety of reasons, whether it be developmental disabilities or mental illness, who are not quite so lucky. Ben is fortunate because he has a community of people who care about him and care to involve him. Ben and others like him often can't advocate for themselves and need others to take notice and care enough to pull them out of isolation. It doesn't even need to involve expensive buildings to be built, or fancy programs to be put into place, because all of Ben's activities are organic, home-grown activities that evolved because people cared to listen to ideas, and say yes to taking a chance on him. His friends, people like Dawn Hochsprung, the principle at Sandy Hook school, who hired Ben to work in the school's library. People like my mom and sister, who took over a social group for young adults with special needs that would have dissolved if they hadn't. People like my husband, who employs not only Ben at his small business, but three or four other young adults with special needs. People like our town Parks and Rec director, who allows our young adults, who are all in their 20s, to use our town's teen center as a place to hang out and gather. People like my daughter, who facilitates that group and also dedicated her career to working with young adults with special needs. And people like that former town staff member, who created a fun and festive gathering for our second-graders. These are all holy moments.

So, going back to the original questions: Why am I still here? What am I supposed to do? I still struggle with these questions, but I'm beginning to wonder if that "something" is simply to continue to do the obvious: live my life, take care of my family, enjoy my friends, teach my students. In other words, to continue to create and to recognize holy moments both small and big, because as Matthew Kelly says, holy moments are contagious, and creating them on a daily basis is what will change the world. Thank you. [*audience applause*]

Cameron: Please welcome Jennifer Hubbard.

Jennifer Hubbard: Given the theme, "Something to start from," the honest truth is that at some point I keep saying, "Today is the day that I'm going to start to grieve." Then one year turns into two, and two into three, and now we're at six. This past December marks a moment where Catherine was alive as long as she lived… or gone, as long as she lived. And what I'm beginning to realize is that something to start from is really nothing — that "something" for me is a moment of abandonment of expectations, and what I thought would be, and a launching into the arms of God, because that "something to start from" is what God wants. And you realize that the "something to start from" was put into place well before December 14th. You see, I had two children at the school. I had Catherine in the first grade and I had Frederick in third grade. What God did with Dawn allowed me to have my son. And that is a gift that I will always thank you for.

Ford: [*barely audible*] It wasn't me.

Hubbard: You see, God's at work in our lives and He has something to start from, because He created us, and the moment we let go of us and let Him follow through with what He started when He knit us together in our mothers' wombs — then the amazing encounters we have with Him blossom and are beautiful. You see, I started my journey with God well before December 14th. I was reunited with God through a friend of Catherine's. I grew up Catholic. I was a cradle Catholic. I knew God, I went to Mass, and somewhere along the way I went to college and abandoned God. I took control of my life, and I thought I was doing the right thing, and saying the right thing, and working at the right career, and I had children. But I stopped all of that and was reunited with God through a little devotional that I would hide, hide in my nightstand, because I didn't want my husband to think that I was some crazy lady. I would read that devotional for the few minutes before Catherine would come home from school — kindergarten was a half-day — and so those few hours while she was at school were prime time. You moms know what I'm talking about — they're the golden hours. I'd spend a few minutes reading this devotional, walk to the bus stop, and I would ponder what I had read. That little devotional led me to the Bible. And I started reading scripture and wondering, What is all this? Then, all of the sudden, Catherine dies, and I wrestled with the question of, "But God, I was just getting to know you, and now what?" Through the course of abandonment, of letting go of expectations, I realized my perfect family in the quintessential town of Newtown, Connecticut, was not exactly how it was all going to end up: we went from four to three in a blink of an eye. What I found was a God who was drawing me in, because that devotional and that Bible were going to carry me through the darkest moments that anybody could ever imagine. We started letting go of expectations, we started letting go of what we thought was right and wrong, and we made our first big choice, which wasn't a really big choice in the scheme of things, you see, people do it every day. You march your kid down to the bus stop, you put your child on the bus, and you send him off to school. You say, "I'll see you when you get home." But for us, that day in January, it was a very real question that we didn't even realize was a question. Would we put our son on the bus and send him to school and put our trust and faith in God and what He had in store for us, or would we take control and bubble wrap him. You see, we were called ahead of time and were told, "You do what you think you need to do, because we don't know what to do. If you want your son to come into school late, or early, or pick him up early, or don't send him at all, we are going to defer to you all." And it wasn't like we had this long conversation, it wasn't a Hollywood moment where the orchestra crescendos, and we walk him down to the bus stop and life continues. It was a guttural reaction of, "No, he must go to school and he's going on the school bus." It was as simple as that, and I truly believe that that's God planting an assurance in our souls to "Put him on the bus, he's mine, and I will take him from there." So that's what we did. We marched him down to the bus stop and we set him off to school. The reality was, he wasn't going to have a good day at school; he wasn't. And the reality was that I couldn't assure him and promise him that he'd be safe; our world had changed. But I did know that I would see him at home. You see, the reality is that I'll see him when he gets home from school, and I will see Catherine when I arrive in heaven. I will never understand why Catherine was taken. I had a lot of living to do with her; man, did I have plans. But it's not for me to understand and I'm okay with that, because God's understanding is far greater, and I know that Catherine's in heaven, I know that I will see her again, I know that there are things that I need to do, starting with being a mom. And that started on that day of sending him back to school and teaching him trust in a Heavenly Father. Without saying "Trust God," I put him on the bus and he went to school, and we went home and wept, and wondered what had we just done. My husband went upstairs and took a shower and said, "If that kid can go to school then I'm going to go to work." In that moment I went downstairs, sat at my kitchen table, and opened up that little devotional. I cracked open the Bible and started reading, because the house was really, really, quiet. Someone had recommended journaling, so I started writing down questions — real and honest questions. I told a girlfriend, "If I ever die, here's where I keep my journals. Please go in the house and burn them [*audience laughter*] because people are going to be angry at me." They were real, honest, and authentic questions of what on earth do I do now, because I have no idea. All expectations and plans were off the table. I started writing. I started reading. All of a sudden, Fr. Peter asked me if I was a writer. I said no, I studied art, and he asked if I would write for *Magnificat*. In those mornings, I would sit at the table and ponder what I would write for *Magnificat*. And if anybody here reads *Magnificat*, you know that there's plenty of times where I talk about the moment when the sun hits the perfect part of the sky, and it pours through my window: I believe it's God reaching down from the heavens and wrapping me in His arms and warming me on those days I feel like I will never be warm again. I'd wake in the middle of the night with answers to what I supposed to write for *Magnificat*. I would write. I would write some more. All of a sudden, I had a purpose.

You see, Catherine loved animals, and so we decided that when we wrote her obituary, we would give donations to our local animal control center. We accidentally left out the word "control," so donations were being sent to a little place called the Animal Center. It was four women, and they called us up after the fact and said, "We received $125,000 in the course of two weeks." And I thought, Are you kidding me? She was six. They came to our kitchen table and said, "We think that what we'd like to do is create an animal sanctuary." I said, "What the heck is an animal sanctuary?" You see, Catherine is the one who loved animals. They explained what the sanctuary was, and they said it's a place where children will see their own innate beauty in the eyes of animals. It's a place of healing, it's a place of peace. As they described it to me, I saw Catherine on the floor, playing, and I saw her spirit delighted in where we would go from here. So we started down this path of building an animal sanctuary, and every single moment that I say, "God, what are you doing? You've picked the wrong person," I'm once again amazed that He would use me, of all people, to create a place where I feel that heaven and earth unite. You see, those moments where I struggle with God are those very days and moments where scripture jumps out at me. Where I am assured that I am His daughter, that I am loved, and there's a purpose for me. That I will be protected, that I will be provided for, and that I will move forward in this life. And you see, that's where something starts. It starts in that moment of abandonment. I look back over the six years and I'm amazed and I'm left in awe, but most importantly, I am humbled that something so beautiful, and something so miraculous as being called the daughter of God can come out of something that is so horrific. [*audience applause*]

Cameron: We have two minutes. So… one question for each. I'm listening to his excellency, Angelo Sala, he's giving me directions. So Dawn, my question for you: About the staff member you were scared of — can we call her? [*audience laughter*]

Ford: She's passed away. [*audience awws*]

187

Cameron: Why do you think she did that?

Ford: Why do I think that she did that? I think that there's something about her that I didn't know. Before, I didn't see a heart in there, but that day I saw a heart in there.

Cameron: I mean, I was just struck by the new beginning that was created through… I mean, your fear, and your being repulsed by her, and whatever. You know, I have dozens of people like this in *my* life. [*audience laughter*] The initiative she took on your behalf changed you. But specifically what changed you? Don't say cupcakes.

Ford: What changed me?

Cameron: Yeah, from what she did.

Ford: My opinion of her. I think that, through that lens, I recognized that people aren't always what you see on the surface, and that we're all struggling with something. I mean, that's really what I thought about her, that maybe she's an unhappy person, and maybe she's struggling with something, but that doesn't mean she doesn't have a heart. I just try to be more patient with people who are maybe cranky. Maybe they have a good heart and they're having a bad day.

Cameron: But I'm also guessing that you gave her a chance to show the world her real heart. I think she took a risk with you.

Ford: Maybe.

Cameron: Jenny: I'm so struck by the courage with which you put Freddy on the bus. Can you say more about that? I mean, where did you ever find that gumption?

Hubbard: I didn't. That's the amazing thing. It didn't come from me. There was…it wasn't even a thought. I was completely at my bottom, my rock-bottom, and I really had nothing. I was on autopilot. I feel like that autopilot was, for me, God. I didn't do anything. I just went with what I thought I was supposed to be doing.

Cameron: But why when you hit rock bottom you didn't just hang out with the rocks?

Hubbard: I don't know. I don't know.

Cameron: You have to know because we brought you here to give us the answer to this question. [*audience laughter*]

Hubbard: I don't know! [*laughs*]

Cameron: Do you think you're insane?

Hubbard: No! [*audience laughter*] I think in every single one of us there is this mustard seed of hope and faith that God does love us. And I think if you have that, God will work with that. I remember praying, "God help me," and I think that's all it takes.

Cameron: Well, this is why you're such a tremendous inspiration to us, and so thank you for taking such a big risk. And Dawn, thank you for the gutsy way that you tell this story. You saved so many lives on that day, but I think even in this room right now, you're doing that. I've heard the story —

Ford: It wasn't me. [*audience laughter*]

Cameron: You need to read Saint Thomas Aquinas on secondary causality. [*audience laughter*] But I'm tellin' ya, I've heard this story before, privately, sitting on your porch, and then once before, on Maiden Lane, and every time I hear it, I just am so moved and want to love God more. And I want to do what you did, in whatever way I can. So thank you all for coming, we hope to see you again.

Born to Never Die

The life of the Servant of God Chiara Corbella. With **Enrico Petrillo**, *Chiara's husband;* **Angelo Carfi**, *Chiara's medical doctor; and moderated by* **Amy Hickl**, *Associate Principal, Notre Dame Academy Elementary School, Los Angeles*

Introduction

Chiara and Enrico married in Italy on September 21, 2008. During the early years of their marriage, the young Italian couple faced many hardships together, including the death of two children, who both died only 30 minutes after birth. Chiara became pregnant a third time with their son, Francesco. However, the joyful news of their pregnancy also came with a fatal diagnosis of cancer for Chiara. Her cancer was an unusual lesion of the tongue, which was later discovered to be a carcinoma. During pregnancy, Chiara rejected any treatment to save her own life if it meant risk to the life of her unborn son. On May 30, 2011, Francesco was born. However, her physical condition worsened. After a year of intense suffering, lived with hope, gladness, and gratitude, Chiara succumbed to cancer on June 13, 2012.

❖   ❖   ❖   ❖   ❖

Amy Hickl: Good evening and welcome. My name is Amy Hickl. I'm the associate principle at an elementary school in Los Angeles, and I'm here to welcome you tonight to a very special evening. We're going to hear a beautiful story. It's the story of Chiara Corbella. It's the story of "Born to Never Die," and we're going to hear the story from these two gentlemen. This is is Enrico Petrillo, he's the husband of Chiara. He is a physical therapist who works in palliative care and lives with his seven-year-old son, Francesco. We're also going to hear tonight from Dr. Angelo Carfi.

Sunday, February 17, 2019

Angelo is married to Elisa and has four children. He is a geriatric doctor who met Chiara and Enrico on the occasion of the funeral of their second child, Davide. He was attracted by their faith, and through their spiritual guide, Fr. Vito, Angelo and Elisa became close friends with Chiara and Enrico. Angelo is also one of the doctors who assisted Chiara until the last hours of her life.

I'm going to turn it over to Angelo now, who's going to tell us Chiara's story.

Angelo Carfi: Good evening, and thank you for inviting us to share this story. It is the story of a woman who had a short life of just 28 years, and a very short marriage of just three and a half years. I apologize — I need to read, otherwise, it will take me too long to go ahead. My English is a little bit sick as you can hear. [*audience laughter*] So, nonetheless I want to do it in English so, Okay. Please, I apologize. [*audience applauds wildly*] What this young woman lived in her life was so incredible that it would take many hours to tell all the story and all that was involved. With Enrico, we decided to take just the parts that are really most important. But we believe that this can touch your hearts very deeply and can also affect your life, so please stay here; we invite you to stay, encourage you to stay, but at your own risk.

Let's just review the facts. Chiara was born in Rome on the 9th of January, 1984. She has a sister called Elisa and her parents are Roberto and Maria Anselma. It's a good family, a very good family. They live close to the Colosseo in Rome, she goes to school, and she has everything. Nonetheless, she develops a very simple spirit and a resolute attitude. She learns how to pray with her mother because they attend a worship group. It is important to say now that Chiara doesn't show any superpower at this time of life. And this is a feature that she will retain until her death and even after, so, she is just one of us. She's just like me and you tonight.

In August of 2002, at the age of 18, she attends a Christian pilgrimage to Medjugorje, which is a place you venerate Mary near Italy, and in this place she meets this guy here, Enrico, and has the intuition that he could become her husband. They fall in love and start to date, and this courtship…yeah, it's a little bit strange but anyway it happened somehow. [*audience laughter*] This courtship will last six years until the 21st of September, 2008, when they will marry in Assisi. It's a very difficult time, a difficult courtship, and Chiara at the very end of the story would refer to it as the hardest part of her life. During this time, they also meet the minor friars in Assisi, including in particular Fr. Vito D'Amato, who becomes their personal spiritual director. Soon after marriage at the age of 24, she becomes pregnant, and during one of the first visits with an ultrasound scanner she is told that the baby has severe malformations involving the brain and would die soon after birth. Enrico and Chiara are just married, but display the exact same attitude towards the baby: she is our daughter, we will accompany her as long as we can. Her name will be Maria Grazia Letizia, which means *Mary, grace,* and *joy.* They also become friends with Chiara's gynecologist, whose name is Daniela, who arranges things for the birth of the baby. Maria Grazia Letizia is born by natural delivery on the 10th of June, 2009, when Chiara is 25 years old. She received the baptism by Fr. Vito directly in the delivery room. Enrico and Chiara spend about half an hour with her in the delivery room and then she dies in their arms. A few days later, during the funeral, the participants experienced words Chiara and Enrico would call a "mysterious joy." They are deeply surprised at what happened with the whole story of Maria Grazia Letizia, and feel simply happy. This is why, soon after Chiara becomes pregnant again, during subsequent tests, they discovered that also this time the baby is sick and would not be suitable for life after birth. They also will do later genetic testing that will verify that the two diseases are completely unrelated to each other.

Enrico and Chiara are ready to accompany this new baby, named Davide Giovanni. This time, however, part of their entourage doesn't accept this and criticizes them bitterly. Davide is born naturally on the 24th of June, 2010, when Chiara is 26, and just like the sister, he is born and baptized in the delivery room and spends his entire earthly life of about half an hour in the arms of his parents. Some days later, his funeral is celebrated, and the participants experience a piece of heaven on earth. Some months later, Chiara is pregnant again, and this time everything is okay with the pregnancy and the child. But a wound develops on the left side of her tongue and doesn't heal. On the 16th of March, 2011, at the age of 27, she needs to undergo surgery to remove this lesion that would be diagnosed as a very aggressive form of cancer. She resolutely decides to postpone all treatments till after the delivery of baby Francesco, because she doesn't want to expose the baby to any risk. The boy is delivered naturally on the 30th of May, 2011. Two days later, she undergoes a surgical revision of the first intervention on the tongue, and lateral neck lymph nodes are removed. Over the following months: tube feeding, radiotherapy on tongue and neck, and chemotherapy. As a consequence, she spends her first months with Francesco unable to talk, unable to swallow, tube-fed with daily radio-therapy sessions and monthly chemotherapies. After the cures, a short time of normal life. But then she develops metastasis in the lung, liver, and muscles, including the right eye motor muscle. On the 4th of April, 2012, she refuses to try a rescue chemotherapy, and in fact invites all her friends on a trip to Medjugorje to ask for a grace. This trip will be attended by nearly 180 friends, and during this trip Chiara will give the testimony of her life that you will see later. She spent the last months of her life in the countryside near Rome, where her family has a house. She's attended by Enrico, Fr. Vito, and her family. On the 13th of June, 2012, after telling all her family members and friends, "I love you," Chiara dies at the age of 28.

I was there on the very day Chiara died, but it is more important for me to tell you how I became friends with Chiara and Enrico. It was because me and my wife were friends of Fr. Vito and Daniela, who told us, "Hey, don't miss the funeral of Davide Giovanni." What? "You missed the first funeral and you don't have to miss the second one." I said it was crazy, it was completely crazy, but yeah, I'll go to this funeral. And what we saw was very, very, peculiar; very strange. There was an atmosphere of joy. There were songs, and you felt joy and love in that time, but I didn't understand, actually. In the middle of the church was the coffin of the baby, a little white coffin. And at the end of the Mass, Enrico and Chiara wanted to make a procession to take the coffin outside the church. And in that moment, Enrico had an uncertainty. He covered his face, and the tears of Enrico were able to open my heart. And I saw, okay, these guys are not religious freaks. Here, the religion is not dumping anything. There's no anesthesia here, there is sheer suffering. These guys are really suffering because they lost their child. So, what is this joy? I understood that no human power could deliver that kind of joy. Someone else was there to deliver it, to give this joy, and so in my heart I started to desire to be involved in that, and we became friends this way.

Now it's time for the video. It is in a digital form, but has the substance of a relic, so we treat in this way. We don't disseminate it on the internet or in the media, because to watch this video you need to meet in person someone who witnessed the story of Chiara. Please turn off everything. Forget about what you have to do next, or who you left at home and cannot attend now. This is a moment for you. Take it for you, because we had to shorten the video a little bit to show it here, and we removed the most emotional parts with the music, all that stuff. It is just for you to see Chiara, and Chiara is telling her story to you now, as she did to her dear friends in Medjugorje.

Video

Hickl: We thank you both so much for letting us hear from Chiara. She passed away two months after that video was taken, so we thank you for the gift of letting us hear from her. Tonight, we also will get to hear from Enrico, with the help of Mark, who will translate for us. So Enrico, we know that every person is an infinite and complex being, but in the video Chiara said you looked at her, you knew her, and you loved her. We would like to hear from you a few of the characteristics about Chiara. In other words, who is Chiara?

Enrico Petrillo: It's not easy to answer because what I know about Chiara is changing. The Lord always does this. He reveals things slowly, not all at once. If I had known during my betrothal that Chiara was like this, a daughter so loved by God, I would have perhaps behaved differently in many situations. But I am the one in the video, I'm the same guy. [*audience laughter*] Chiara was, as you saw, a beautiful woman, a beautiful girl, luminous, joyful. The more I know her, the more I know that the center of her life is Another. The way I see it, Chiara is a daughter, simply a daughter of God, that has lived everything that the Father allowed to happen in her life, made happen in her life lifted as a daughter. I've had the grace, the chance to see Chiara die. It was a terrible day but also a most beautiful day. To see Chiara die allowed me to see how a daughter of God dies.

We cannot die happy, yet I saw Chiara die happy. How is it possible? It is only possible if we have a relationship that we call faith. To have that relationship — as Angelo was saying before, she was not a a superwoman. It's simply like this: Chiara is a daughter, simply like you are. And I have no doubt that this grace is a gift God wants to give me and also to you. And so, what I hope happens in your heart is that you don't make of Chiara a saint that you put on the altar, because all of you, each of you, is called to the same thing. To experiment, to live your sonship, your daughtership. All these events are nothing more than a discovery of a journey to rediscover your daughtership, your sonship, with Him. What we have discovered is that God was waiting for us exactly there, in and within our limits. Yes, you have to accept your limits. I've met here in these days people with superior intelligence; I'm not that intelligent. Not even Chiara. But with intelligence one cannot become a son or a daughter. There's no way that man can generate himself this sonship or daughtership; only a Father can. We can accept, we can welcome that life that He has already given us. I saw Chiara die happy because she is a daughter. I often think these days of the people of Israel, who had mountains to their left and right, and behind them the whole Egyptian army. At a certain point they even have the sea in front of them and there's no escape, they are completely imprisoned, stuck like we are. Sooner or later we will get sick and we will die. We have to experience that limit, but if we live it in relationship with Him, we will make it. Amen. [*audience applause*]

Hickl: Follow up question: If Chiara is not a superwoman, if she was just a woman who made a journey to know that she was a daughter of God, can you tell us how you made that journey together while she was sick, and what helps you face your limits?

Petrillo: We began to meet the Lord individually. We met in Medjugorje, already converted, and on a path to discover and learn about the Lord. And so, by walking simply, the Lord teaches you many things. You begin to learn to recognize them in your story, in your personal story, in the events of your life. God speaks in this way. Neither Chiara nor I had ever seen the Virgin Mary or the Lord. The story is of us walking towards Him. He will teach us, He will show us. I have a son, Francesco, who's now seven years old. As a father, I cannot wait for him to understand how much I love him. It's like that with God. He cannot wait for us to become aware, to recognize how much He loves us. It's our story itself that taught us that. Our children, with such short lives, they taught us to die. To see these two kids, these two babies, die, was very beautiful. They simply fell asleep and they went directly to the Lord. There was nothing ugly about it. We really thought with Chiara that the day of our death would be the most beautiful day of our lives, because finally we will understand everything. The Lord makes us walk in our story with the things that He proposes. Too often we complain that, well, we didn't have parents like Chiara had, we didn't have a husband like Chiara had, we didn't have a spiritual director like Fr. Vito. If, if, if. If things had been different, I would have behaved differently, if things were different, it would have been well. But life is written with the *yes*, not with the *if*. Chiara had a beautiful gift: the capacity to give space to grace. This capacity to allow herself to be loved. Thanks to the lives of our children, we have understood that the only thing important in life is to let yourself be loved. We live in a Christianity today that is often, too often, something to do, things to do. We delude ourselves with thinking that by doing things we will arrive at God, but it's not like that. We are like the Hebrews, who thought that by washing their hands they'll be closer to God. We understand now that it's not like this. Our experience is the experience of an Easter. We have to live already in this way. If you are, if you are son or daughter, you are already risen. Chiara lived like that, everything that happened in her life, knowing that whatever happens, I'll make it because the Lord is with me.

Hickl: You and Chiara learned these beautiful things through suffering. We live in a culture that says you have to do everything possible to *avoid* suffering. Can you tell us what suffering is for you?

Petrillo: These things have been learned through blood and tears and flesh, and that's why they're real. Chiara is truly dead, she died truly. But even when we were betrothed, we were engaged, we were talking about the Lord in this way. Nobody believed us. Yet, Chiara has died, and with her blood we actually even made it to America. We are very much afraid of suffering; Chiara didn't love it. Yet we discovered that in the cross we have a great occasion, a great opportunity, which is that of being able to be more intimate, to speak more intimately with the Lord. I often think of Jesus on the cross with the two thieves. Only the thieves were speaking with Jesus. When you're in pain, when you're suffering, you have the privilege of being able to speak more intimately with the Lord if you want. And that's the way it was for us, for Chiara. When Chiara was dying, in my heart I heard this phrase of the Lord: "My yoke is easy and my burden light." But when I was seeing her dying, I could not see, I was not able to see that sweetness. That morning I asked her — it was her last morning, she was in the wheelchair praying in front of the tabernacle that we had the grace to have in our house for the last two months, because by that time Fr. Vito was living with us. While she was praying, I came close to her and asked her this: "Is it truly sweet, this cross of the Lord?" And she answered, smiling, "Yes, it is very sweet."

I know that Chiara is very much a loved daughter; she was and still is. But I'm here to say that you are, too. And also for you the cross will be sweet. You saw Chiara in the video asking the Lord to have the grace to welcome grace. Grace happens in the present. She didn't have grace only the day before she died, she had grace the day, the moment she died. And Jesus is not a liar. Grace will come at the right moment and the sea will be open and the Hebrews will pass.

Hickl: One more question. The title of the event says that we are born to never die, so can you describe for us your relationship with Chiara now? We know it's different, but how is she present to you now?

Petrillo: My relationship with Chiara now is that I have no relationship with Chiara now. I'm a widow. Sincerely, I never looked, searched for a relationship with her now, now that she's dead. I have no doubt that she is close to me, that she prays for me, and for Francesco our son. I know that she's happy now and I'm happy for her. For my life right now, Chiara is a star that guides, that shines on my path, indicates my path. We talk about her life, not to just remember her, but because her memory helps us to live. Her memory allows me to know the path of my life, whether I'm going the right direction or not. The same way we do when we read the Gospel, we remember what the Lord did. That is my relationship with her today. It's a light that was chosen by God, illuminates my life and my road, my path. And I hope to continue following this path that has been traced for me. Amen.

Hickl: Amen. [*audience applause*]

Petrillo: One last thing. I think that you are my relationship with Chiara today, because you are a great consolation for me. Thank you.

Hickl: We thank both of you so much. You said at the beginning, Angelo, that Chiara was not a superwoman, that she's the same as us, so I want to just finish with a quote from Fr. Giussani about the saints. He said, "The saint is not a superman. The saint is a true man. The saint is a true man because he adheres to God and thus to the ideal for which his heart has been made and of which his destiny consists." And you've witnessed that to us tonight, so we thank you. [*audience applause*]

Riro Manuscalco: Thank you, Enrico. Thank you, Angelo. Thank you, Chiara. And thank you to each one of you. The Encounter is an act of gratitude — it's a grace. You being here is also an act of gratitude. It's not by chance that these things happen. There's grace, there's a gift. We started with that question: "Has anyone ever promised us anything?" Well, we can say yes. Yes. And in these days, we've had so many testimonies. The promise can be fulfilled. Probably not according to our images, not according to what we have in mind, but it will be fulfilled. And as Enrico said, it will be sweet. We will close with an excerpt from a letter we received from a friend in Venezuela, who was here with us maybe two years ago, and you know the situation there.

"I pictured the uncertainty the disciples faced after Jesus' death, the predicament. The only difference is that our great certainty, the great certainty in our lives, is the Resurrection. The Resurrection dating back 2,000 years that we can still experience today. Christ is the key today for seeing all things as new. Responding to what will happen is just a political analysis that cannot solve this morning's predicament. To me, the most reasonable stand is that of Saint Benedict: to pray and work wherever and however it is possible. Each of us with their task, always striving to help one another to live as a community because He is our hope. Thank you."